D0040918

More Advance Praise for *CEO Material*

"*Excellent book. It is very useful for anyone interested in succeeding at work or at home. Debra Benton is the best at distilling useful information.*"

—CURT CARTER, CEO, America, Inc.

"*I classify* CEO Material *as a business bible and not just a book sold on the shelf. This information is reality and this is how you change.*"

—LAURENCE SALMON, CEO, Mazrui Holdings in United Arab Emirates

"*Debra Benton has found a way to expose what lies below the surface of the murky waters of leadership development.* CEO Material *is a great book for everyone regardless of the stage of their career.*"

—CHRISTI PEDRA, CEO, Siemens Hearing Instruments

"*I've always had this notion that entrepreneurs bred entrepreneurs. You can learn this stuff, people! This book is a must read if you are serious about making an impact on your life, the company you work for and on the world for that matter. Even if you're already sitting at the top, listening to advice from so many other CEOs is pretty powerful stuff. Read it twice!*"

—ROBBIN PHILLIPS, courageous president, Brains on Fire

"*I wish I had this roadmap earlier in my life. I might have been more successful sooner! You have nailed it. Very, very good advice from the front row seat of what does and does not work.*"

—TED WRIGHT, CEO and president, Setai Hotels and Resorts, LLC

"*Love [for what you do], education, attitude, determination, enthusiasm, responsibility, spirituality, humor, integrity, perception = leadership—this book has it all.*"

—RICHARD RUSH, CEO and president, State Chamber of Oklahoma

"When life calls for an upgrade—to first class—Benton's charming wisdom is your ticket. She will help you beyond belief."

—MATTHEW J. BENNETT, CEO, First Class Flyer, Inc.

"Having spent a lifetime in the fire service, I learned through tough experience the lessons of leadership. Sharing those lessons with others, and learning how much the same it is for all leaders, is invaluable."

—KATE DARGAN, state fire marshall, California

"Benton's clarity on the critical attributes of top-notch leaders offers aspiring executives a roadmap to success."

—STEPHEN B. BONNER, CEO and president,
Cancer Treatment Centers of America

CEO
MATERIAL

CEO

MATERIAL

HOW TO BE A LEADER IN ANY ORGANIZATION

D. A. BENTON

New York   Chicago   San Francisco   Lisbon   London   Madrid   Mexico City
Milan   New Delhi   San Juan   Seoul   Singapore   Sydney   Toronto

The McGraw·Hill Companies

Copyright © 2009 by D. A. Benton. All rights reserved. Printed in the United States of America. Except as permitted under the United States Copyright Act of 1976, no part of this publication may be reproduced or distributed in any form or by any means, or stored in a database or retrieval system, without the prior written permission of the publisher.

1 2 3 4 5 6 7 8 9   DOC/DOC   0 1 0 9

ISBN   978-0-07-160545-8
MHID   0-07-160545-2

McGraw-Hill books are available at special quantity discounts to use as premiums and sales promotions or for use in corporate training programs. To contact a representative, please visit the Contact Us pages at www.mhprofessional.com.

Library of Congress Cataloging-in-Publication Data

Benton, D. A. (Debra A.)
       CEO Material : How to be a leader in any organization / by D. A. Benton.
          p. cm.
       Includes bibliographical references and index.
       ISBN 0-07-160545-2 (alk. paper)
     1. Leadership. 2. Executive ability. 3. Success. I. Title.

       HD57.7.B4665   2009
         658.49092—dc22   2008050316

With extraordinary thanks to Rodney, Fred, and Teresa—who taught me not only how to make a living, but also how to live.

Contents

Note from D. A. Benton

THE REAL AUTHORS of this book include
Carlos Alvarez, CEO, Gambrinus
Rick Ambrose, General Manager, Surveillance and Navigational
    Systems, Lockheed Martin
Carol Ballock, Group Lead Corporate/Financial Practice, Burson-
    Marstellor
Thoko Bando, poet
Jimmy Barge, EVP, Controller, Tax & Treasury, Viacom
Bob Berkowitz, Principal, Dilenschneider Group
John Bianchi, President, Frontier Gunleather
Stuart Blinder, CEO, Insight Consulting
Karen Bohler, President, Bohler Institute
Daryl Brewster, CEO, Krispy Kreme Doughnut Corporation
John Butler, EVP Human Resources, Pinnacle Foods
Ivan Campuzano, CEO, Howtogetyourshineon.com
Curtis Rex Carter, CEO, America, Inc.
Linda Childears, President, Daniels Fund
Doug Conant, CEO, Campbell Soup Company
Susan M. Copperman, VP, HSM
Midge Cozzens, Director, Knowles Science Teaching Foundation
Caroline Creager, CEO, Executive Physical Therapy

Mindy Credi, VP Human Resources, Sears Roebuck & Co.

Gayle Crowell, Advisor, Warburg Pincus Venture Capital

Bill Coleman, CEO, Cassatt Corporation

Mac Cook, President, Mac Daddy Enterprises

Pamela Kreegor Cook, President, PSK Inc.

Karen Cox, CEO, KJC Solutions, Inc.

Jeffrey M. Cunningham, Publisher, Directorship

Ralph Dahman, Managing Director, Galderma Australia/
New Zealand

Kate Dargan, State Fire Marshall, California

Tim Day, CEO, Bar-S Food

Harry Devereaux, President, Home State Bank

Maury Dobbie, CEO, NCEDC

Brian Fabes, CEO, Civic Consulting Alliance

Jack Falvey, CEO, Makingthenumbers.com

Mike Fernandez, VP Public Affairs, State Farm

Mick Fleming, CEO, American Chamber of Commerce Executives

Tricia Fox, Director, HumanResources, Quaker, Tropicana, &
Gatorade

Pam Forbus, Director of Innovation, Frito-Lay

Bradley Fortin, CEO, Maverick Systems Group, LLC

Dale Fuller, CEO, McAfee, Inc.

Kent Gale, CEO, Market Intelligence Leaders

Mike Gass, President & CEO, United Launch Alliance

Ilana Goldman, President, Women's Campaign Forum

Jim Goldman, President & CEO, Godiva Chocolatier

Dave Hardie, Managing Director, Herbert Mines Associates

Heidi O. Hart, CEO, Pretty Brainy

Jerry Henry, CEO, Johns Manville Corporation

Kent Heyman, Chairman & CEO, Migo Software, Inc.

Kerry Hicks, CEO, Healthgrades

Steve Hochhauser, President of Security Technologies, Ingersoll
Rand Security

Brian Seth Hurst, CEO, Opportunity Management, Inc.

Charles Ingersoll, Sr., Client Partner, Korn/Ferry

Carl Johnson, Senior VP, Campbell Soup Company

Hal Johnson, Managing Director, Client Development, Korn/Ferry
Sean J. Johnstone, Group Leader, Kawada Industries, Inc.
Chet Kapoor, CEO, Sonoa Systems
Kelvin Kessler, M.D.
Larry Kopp, CEO, Globe Capital
John Krebbs, CEO, PACO, Inc.
Natalie Laackman, CFO, Best Kosher Foods Corp.
Chris Kubasik, EVP, Lockheed Martin Electronic Systems
Marshall Kuykendall, President, Kuykendall Land Co.
Hunt Lambert, Director, Center for Entrepreneurship, CSU
Lawrence Land, Attorney
Larry Lawson, EVP & General Manager, Lockheed Martin
    Aeronautics Corporation
Cynthia Liebrock, CEO, Easy Access to Health, LLC
Christopher G. Lis, SVP Research & Development, Cancer
    Treatment Centers of America
Filemon Lopez, Regional Senior VP, Comcast
Ted Leovich, CEO, Global Brand Consulting
Steve Mabry, SVP, AXA Equitable
Peter Mannetti, Managing Partner, iSherpa Venture Capitalist
Reuben Mark, Chairman of the Board, Colgate-Palmolive
David May, CEO, Ft. Collins Chamber of Commerce
Anne McCarthey, Dean, University of Baltimore, Merrick School
    of Business
Bob McCluskey, State Representative—Colorado
James Mead, President, CEO, James Mead & Company
Amanda Mellos, Associate, Benton Management Resources, Inc.
Steve Milovich, SVP Corporate HR, Walt Disney Company
Sam Morse, VP, SOS-Tech Maintenance Company
Deanna Mulligan, President, DMM Management Solutions, LLC
Dan Munroe, VP Life Insurance Product Development,
    AXA Equitable
Mike Nieset, Managing Director, Heidrick and Struggles
Osman Oerer, Managing Director, Enterprise Consulting Corp., AG
Art Oldham, CEO, Oldham Planning and Design
Jim Ostrosky, Co-President, USC Consulting

Stan Payne, CEO, Canaveral Port Authority
Jon Peters, President, Institute for Management Studies
Janine and Craig Petersen, Co-CEOs, Southwestern Arts
Joe Petrone, VP Human Resources, Lockheed Martin Electronics
Robbin Phillips, CEO, Brains on Fire
Hal Pittman, Director Public Affairs, U.S. Joint Forces Command
Gene Pope, VP IT, Corp. Service, VP Developer Service,
    Amazon
Dave Powelson, Private Investor
Glenn Reed, EVP Engineering & Operations, Approach Resources
Mary Reed, CEO, Hauldren Group
Darcy Rezac, Managing Director & Chief Engagement Officer,
    The Vancouver Board of Trade
Randy Rodriquez, CEO, Rio Bravo
David Rome, CEO, Rome Antics
Laurence Salmon, CEO, Equilect Capital, Inc.
Mark Sarvary, CEO, Tempur-Pedic, Inc.
Al Schorre, District Attorney, Midland, Texas
Michael Schriver, President, Duty Free Shops Group Limited
Markus Schweig, VP Technology & Chief Architect, Smith and
    Tinker, Inc.
Michael Scott, writer
Jim Sears, President, A2BE Carbon Capture
Paul Schlossberg, CEO, D/FW Consulting
Sandra Shoemaker, VP Enterprise Resources Manager, Lockheed
    Martin Aeronautics
Ed Shonsey, CEO, HR Biopetroleum
Norm Singer, EVP, Sage Canyon Investment Advisors, LLC
John Slagle, CEO, Slagle & Associates
Dr. Jamie Smiell, Executive Director Clinical Research &
    Development, Celgene
Rulon Stacey, President & CEO, Poudre Valley Health Systems
S. Frederick Starr, Chairman, Central Asia Caucasus Institute
    at John Hopkins University
Lu Stasko, CEO, The Stasko Agency
Jim Striggow, CEO, The Rock Garden

Richard Storck, CEO, Storck Development
Hugh Sullivan, CEO, Sullivan Group
Rudy Tauscher, General Manager, Mandarin Oriental
Richard Tait, Founder, Cranium, Inc.
Richard Torrenzano, CEO, Torrenzano Group
Michael Trufant, CEO, G&M Marine, Inc.
Donna Uchida, CEO, Skyhill Group
Matthew Villalobos, CEO, TMB Creative
Cathinka Wahlstrom, Partner, Accenture
Wynn Willard, CMO, Cott Corporation
Rob Woodard, VP Global Consumer & Customer Insights,
    Campbell Soup Company
Ted Wright, President & CEO, Setai Hotel & Resorts, LLC
Dennis Wu, CFO, United Commercial Bank
Joe Zimlick, CEO, Bohemian Foundation

CEO
MATERIAL

Introduction:
You Are CEO Material If...

RIGHT NOW—*WHERE YOU WORK*—there are people behind closed doors desperately trying to find someone to promote or develop for a larger role. When your name comes up, you want one of those authoritative-looking people to speak up and say, "[Your name here] is someone we're watching— we need a half dozen more like [your name here]. He [or she—it goes without saying!] could be a leader in any organization...*real CEO material.*"

"Why do you think so?" someone in the room asks.

"Well, he is a first-rate performer who makes others glow brighter around him. He is so honest you could play cards with him on the phone. He's not afraid to make big decisions, take risks, or make mistakes because he learns from everything he's involved in and applies it to the next time. He fits in with our way of doing things yet can step up and stand out when necessary. He attracts the best people around him. He doesn't shoot his mouth off. He has consistently had progressively more complex work on an accelerated basis. He has developed two or three people who could step in and fill his void when he moves up. He is insatiably curious about stuff that is not just directly related to his job. He enjoys a solid and supportive home life. People like him, trust him, and will walk off the edge of the earth for him. And he's a leader in every situation he's been in. *That's* why."

A 36-second statement like this, said by the right person at the right time, can propel you to the top. But remember, it only takes one of these two-second statements to sink you: "He lies." "She doesn't listen." "He blames others." "She demeans her team."

A lot of organizations have formal guidelines using a proficiency model to evaluate and advance people around job experience, emotional competencies, interpersonal skills, decision making, and leadership style. But *all* organizations have informal, colloquial, anecdotal, abstract, idiosyncratic, and not-well-constructed methods to evaluate and advance people.

People like to think that adhering to the formalized six steps or seven tenets provided by human resources and sent out to every employee in a four-color brochure will ensure their advancement. But that's unrealistic. It's not that neat and direct. In fact, it's muddy, murky, and amorphous.

Personal opinions by people of influence are formed, spoken and unspoken, on what you do and how you behave in the tangible *and* intangible areas. Every move is observed. Fewer actions go unnoticed than you'd like to believe. And honestly, by most C-suite executives' admission, the informal trumps the formal.

Note to readers: All italicized quotes in this book come verbatim from a conversation with one of the CEOs I spent time with.

Conversations go on continuously trying to fill gaps and deficits in our people.

It's not a pool to choose from, more like a puddle. We're talent starved.

First, you are separated on performance, but there are a lot of good performers. The differentiating beyond that gets messy.

In our formal system you're evaluated on the results you deliver and how you did it against company criteria of character, competence, and ability to thrive in a team-based environment. And that's true for internal candidates as well as people from the outside. Search

firms we use follow the criteria we've established that fits our culture. ...But if I put myself through the company's criteria, I would have failed.

Below the VP level people don't realize how much of this type of conversation is going on. People are evaluating you all the time with a limited set of information, infrequent interaction, often from second- and third-hand information. That's just the reality. And as you move up, people below you are evaluating you just the same.

People will say it doesn't happen this way, but it does.

If you are looking to bust through from supervisor to manager, manager to division head, division head to vice president, vice president to senior vice president, and senior vice president to CEO or from a small organization to a big one—every stage is about differentiation.

For every 5 formal qualifiers, there are 30 disqualifiers, and they can be almost anything and everything.

You need to know both. Every chapter in this book discusses the qualifiers (tangible and intangible) that, if you ignore them, become a disqualifier. The formal depends on the process your company has laid out, which you have to pay attention to, as well as the informal: "What are her warts?" "Is he going to lose weight?" "Did she quit smoking?" "How is his spouse with this?"

My goal is to separate out the messiness and help you to anticipate and understand those intangibles. It's like a renowned interior home designer who explained aesthetic design, "It's not the color of the walls that makes a difference but the color of the air in the room."

Let me make it clear: You do not need to be the company's record-producing individual performer to be talked about in a glowing manner. You do not have to be an alumnus of a blue-chip company, a graduate from a top B-school, or have the highest IQ. You do not have to have been the fastest kid in the class or the smartest in math. And you do not need to have a "leader" gene in your DNA.

You can come from any walk of life. You can be tall, short, attractive, not so attractive, smart, or not so smart.

It's easier than you think to be a stellar leader. Whether you are trapped in a male or a female body, you can be a leader in any organization—and not just a typical chief but a terrific one. It's going to happen to someone; it might as well be you.

Even if your current job is being the person who *gets* the coffee for the person who *makes* the coffee, you can take on the ownership of your career the minute you start reading this book. If you don't take hold of your work life, you'll blink your eyes one day and say, "What the heck happened in the last 2 or 22 years?"

If you do not stay on top of your business life, you'll get older faster than you'll get better or wiser. In 365 days, you will have added another year to your age. *Or* in 365 days, you will have added that year *with* heightened confidence, improved leadership expertise, and real opportunities for promotion. Either way, you'll wake up, and the time will pass when "nothing has changed" unless you do something unprecedented in your work life, starting now to get *pulled up from above and simultaneously pushed up from below.* The good news is that it's all doable by you—and it's worth it.

Your boss, your boss's boss, the human resources department, and headhunters are not your career managers—you are. Now, sometimes their endeavors benefit you, but if you wait for that impetus, you might wait forever. They organize their efforts and resources around their needs, not yours. They do not concern themselves as to whether you choose to be a "B-player" or "assistant-to" for the rest of your life.

Unwavering desire, unshakable focus, and consistent effort are all it takes. Believe me, it's not nearly as hard as being an NFL quarterback, professional pitcher, chart-topping singer, Olympic medal winner, or ironman triathlete.

Scientific researchers say that it takes people around 10 years minimum to excel in a field, whether it is brain surgery or selling computers. That is, *if* during those years you put in 10,000 hours of deliberate practice. A back-of-the-envelope calculation breaks 10 years and 10,000 hours down to 1,000 hours a year (19 hours a week) or 2.7 hours a day of deliberate practice required to excel. (Ironman athletes, for example, put in, on average, 6.4 hours a day.) Being an exemplary leader is doable by you.

You're working those 3 hours a day anyway; that effort might as well be the most fruitful deliberate action toward the goal you want.

This is what to do at 22 to be a top dog by 42.

CEO Material is the set-the-record-straight framework garnered from a group of top dogs (or you can call them *thought leaders*) talking about what it takes today. (By reading this, I want you to be yourself, but their advice helps you to shape yourself.) You'll recognize some of what you know to do already, and you can check off, "Yes, I do that." You'll also see what you need to work on, noting, "I've got to do more of that."

Treat it like a game. Find out the rules, and figure out how to play to win.

The first law: Understand the rules, but play your own game. The second law: Understand the rules, but play your own game. The third law: Understand the rules, but play your own game.

You make it yours, but there is a foundation.

Every organization needs a leader. Motorcycle gangs have (official and unofficial) designated leaders, as do Red Cross workers. Children on school playgrounds follow the leader, just like dogs do in a pack. Regardless of your calling, someone is going to lead the charge; no group can do without. Again, it might as well be you.

In business, they're formally called *chief* (fill in the blank with *operating, technical, legal, personnel, administrative, technology, information, continuity, risk, nuclear, marketing, manufacturing, financial, purchasing, quality, country, security, learning,* or *strategic*) *officer*—which can lead to the CEO.

Being that person (with the formal title or not) is a lot bigger rush than base jumping. It's rad. It's cool. And it's awesome.

Everyone wants to be a chief, but most feel it's unrealistic, so they turn it around and act like they don't want it anyway. But they wouldn't turn it down if offered.

Over many conversations with a number of CEOs, I asked why being a leader is a good gig. They told me that you have the best chance of any job in the organization to

- Turn things around, make things happen.
- Be the coach, the mentor.
- Make a difference.
- Get to select the people you're around.
- Be able to do something about the problems you complain about.
- Make your own decisions.
- Minimize doing things that you think are stupid.
- Choose the chances you're going to take.
- Make decisions that can change the world.
- Be able to help more people.
- Do what you think is right.
- Be the boss you always wanted to have.
- And control your own destiny.

The fact is that being a leader in any organization is a most noble (and interesting) job. What's more important than working as the big kahuna to build an organization, putting wages in peoples' pockets, growing the economy, and making the world a better place?

I figured I'm as smart as others running the show. I decided to be the boss that I always wanted to have.

Plus, you'll make from 40 to 1,000 times more money than what most people make in their first job. Now, if that offends you, it's something you can change once you're in the top seat.

Money doesn't buy happiness, but you can look for it in much nicer places.

Also, as the leader, chief, or CEO, you have the most direct route to help humanity. In addition to leading the organization as you see fit, as a head you can take on a socially responsible position to direct resources toward solutions in global climate change, energy challenges, clean water in developing countries, the world economy, global peace, chronic hunger and poverty, humanitarian relief, corruption, West Islamic world dialogue, information technology (IT) access for everyone, wellness and health issues (e.g., HIV, malaria, etc.), education initiatives, and at the very least, an equal opportunity for people to grow and prosper.

"You can pair self-interest that is the hallmark of capitalism with interest in the welfare of others," says Bill Gates, chairman of the board of Microsoft, speaking at Davos (who put $33 billion into his foundation to improve health care worldwide).

This kind of stewardship is a gift not many people get to have. You need initiative, influence, and resources to do what Gates promotes—and that can come only from being a leader.

You know what *you're* about: ambitious, technologically adept, adaptable, civic-minded, socially conscious, success-driven, unafraid to question the status quo, confident, a multitasker, and generally optimistic. You already have the foundation of what makes up leadership; you might as well go all the way.

If you're reading this and you think, "Oh, I don't want to work in a big company. I want to do my own thing, start my own business, be the boss—the CEO—from the start." Fine. Good for you. You know what you want, so everything in this book is all the more important for you. Each aspect of producing results, being a generalist, self-development, confidence, integrity, developing others, communicating, getting and staying connected, being decisive, and keeping balance to lead are demanded of you, but sooner. No, immediately!

Venture capitalists tell me that they see, on average, 1,000 business plans a year and invest in 8. The 8 are chosen as much for the idea as the CEO and his or her leadership skills. If you choose to ignore any part presented in this book, you risk working for a jerk—if you're self-employed.

An important thing to realize is that you can home school yourself on being a leader instead of waiting for any big organization's institutional rigor to click in. In fact, you *can't* wait. Starting today, take on your own authority to think and act like the owner, the top boss, the CEO; do it regardless of your current job and title. Do it for yourself, your family, your career, your future, your organization, your team, your life, and your legacy.

Public companies, on average, replace their top leaders every five years, according to the search firm, Spencer Stuart. (This is much lower than the average NFL team, with turnover of almost 40 percent every year.) With 76 million baby boomers leaving the workforce across the board, people will be promoted to bigger jobs earlier (this is happening in Europe and Asia too). The fact is that 92 percent of the 350 million people in this country will end up working at some job level in corporate America. I say that if you're going to end up enrolled there anyway, you might as well go for the best job starting now, and that is a role of leadership.

The Truth from Successful Leaders on How *You* Can Become One Too

I've spent 30 years consulting with, coaching, being mentored by, studying, and hanging out with CEOs of all types. Despite any downside to the top job (as there is in every job), the ones who are there wouldn't want to be anywhere else.

To write this book, I called on a global group of 100+ CEO contacts who've been mentors, sponsors, and clients over the years. Five hours a day for seven months, I sat down and talked with them to get new-age and age-old life and career management advice.

A Google search of "what is leadership" pulls up over 102 million listings. Although a lot is written about the subject, only a little literally comes from the "horse's mouth." Over the years, I've discovered that's how I like to learn—to shadow (not stalk, mind you!), go where they go, do what they do, witness how they think, observe what their professional and personal lives are about; and ask lots of questions about their experiences and their lessons learned and earned. Every bit of helpful knowledge I gathered, I want to pass on to you.

We discussed their thoughts on career advancement, life principles, business theory, and recent scientific study in psychological, economic, and organizational behavior. I asked what gets their attention as far as "up and comers." What do they know now that sure would have helped them in their own climb. And how to facilitate being the one favorably talked about behind closed doors.

Frequently, they prefaced answers with, "What I tell my own children is..." or "What I learned from my mentors..." or "What I wish someone had told me was...." The recommendations I present in this book come from CEO consensus on various issues, and I've included lots of their direct quotes that are highlighted to emphasize a point.

The advice I give my grandson is "every horse kicks, every mule bites, all guns are loaded, and every second guy you meet is a fool."

The CEOs are from public and private Fortune 50 to Fortune 5000 companies headed up by professional "guns for hire," entrepreneurs, and SOBs (sons of bosses). They are dot-com billionaires, financial service providers, defense contractors, food service companies, manufacturers of products from computer disks to breast implants, and several serial entrepreneurs. With some I got 30 minutes; others gave me hours and even days to "shadow" them, examine, and query at length. (Sometimes, when top dogs talk about what it takes to get to the top, they just don't stop!)

For secondary source material, I sat down with their CEO friends and some of their spouses (first, second, or more and a few life partners), sometimes their children (natural, adopted, and step), at their homes (lofts, seaside villas, mini-mansions, penthouse condos, mountain lodges, or custom-made double-wides) or; in or on their vehicle of choice (sailboats, motor boats, lobster boats, Gulfstreams, NetJets, or Beechcraft Baron). Sometimes I was invited to attend church with them, family reunions, class reunions, company picnics, and executive off-sites. My husband and I have been bicycling, hiking, camping, hunting, fishing, and kayaking with some of them. (They don't just sit behind a desk and watch the stock ticker!)

Obviously, there were fun experiences I personally enjoyed, but my main focus was always to extract every ounce of learning possible. My goal from each encounter was to provide the most beneficial information available from those who have "been there, done that, and bought the T-shirt." (You can't get this stuff from surveys.)

From those structured (and some not so structured) conversations, you'll acquire suggestions they received from their own mentors and sponsors, rules they established for themselves, and ways they accelerated their career; you'll find out darn good, practical information that works for them so that you can incorporate it into what will work for you.

Many of the things they spoke about were as a mentor to me rather than from a corporate or policy position. To relay relevant information, get the full color and context of their content, but not go "on the record" with attribution, I use, "One CEO said..." and more frequently I just differentiate the quote from the body of the text like the one that follows.

> *D.A., you quoted me in one of your books. Although, I liked seeing my name in print when perusing the book stores, people thought I was speaking corporate policy when I was just trying to provide some inside insight. Plus, I received way too many résumés with people using my words back to me in their cover letter....You know I'm always willing to talk to you and try to be of help to your readers, so now I'd be grateful if it's not directly attributed.*

I agreed because my goal was (1) to have the CEOs feel comfortably candid; (2) to include everything of value to be of help to you; (3) to provide highly confidential, frank, and honest advice; and (4) to have it feel like you and I and a bunch of CEOs were sitting around at a barefoot beachside bar (or at lunch at the Trump) chatting as friends thinking along with them. Some quotes are attributed because they are a matter of public record. Regardless, it doesn't matter which specific CEO said what exact words. What matters is that their advice and recommendations are more similar than dissimilar and strikingly doable—and they are willing to pass it on to you.

This book will dissect and explain realistic evaluation standards for the leadership foursome of craftsmanship, confidence, constant communication, and collaboration with coworkers—all needed to be called a "trailblazer,"... "groundbreaker,"... "firefighter,"... "rainmaker,"... "water walker,"... or "slammer," in those closed-door management development meetings.

My goal for you reading this book is that it's a vehicle for your steep "free climb" up the vertical business world where there are no fixed paths and no fixed rules. My wish is that you, my reader,

- Evolve as a person.
- Learn about the world.

- Reduce any damaging impact.
- Climb in the best style possible.
- Share experiences with others.
- Undergo an adventure all your own.

Warren Buffett says that he wished he'd started investing at an earlier age than he did. (He started when he was six years old.) Wherever you are in your career, it's not too late or too early to put things in place for your future. Where you are today is a product of your past decisions. Where you will be in the future is a product of today's decisions. The following is to help you with your decisions. So what are you waiting for?

1

You Have a Good Track Record

- Generate work for yourself.
- Work innovatively and imaginatively.
- Develop people relationships

It is an obvious requirement to produce the right results — *that add value to the organization* — on time, under budget, and without a "hassle" factor. This is necessary but not sufficient to having a track record that receives raves in talent planning meetings.

You also have to enable, help, and guide other people (whether part of your own team or not) to achieve similar results. Your track record is not just about you and your business potency: It's the specialty you excel in, what you take on beyond what others do, and the connections you initiate with people outside your immediate circle in the way of contacts, mentors, and sponsors.

> *Focus on the things you can control, and at the end of the day, the only thing you can control is your performance.*

When I babysat as a teen, my parents taught me to do the dishes, laundry, and clean the house too. I was the most sought out and heavily tipped babysitter in town.

Executive search professionals from Korn/Ferry, Spencer Stuart, and Russell Reynolds unanimously say, "The best predictor of the future is the past." So it's a requisite to have a history of triumphal outcomes to be seen as a potential potentate.

Do good work preferably in revenue-driving functions such as sales, marketing, operations, and finance (where most corporate leaders come from; few come from human resources, so don't have that as your only expertise). Over time, get experience in human resources, though, as well as turnaround, startup, joint-venture, or venture-capital exposure as fits your company.

Whether you are an engineer, an accountant, a salesperson, a computer guru, or a marketing wizard—it's all fine as long as you continually get progressively challenging assignments and demonstrate competency and an ability to oversee, stimulate, and nurture people.

When you are "chief," you will be judged on your ability to positively affect the stock price, find growth opportunities, provide shareholder profitability, increase sales, provide return on investment, increase market share, and improve employees. Whatever you can do today in whatever job you have to make some impact on any of these areas demonstrates "the past that will predict your future."

The white space between candidates is very small, particularly the higher up you go. You need to be really good at something important that adds value to the company—in the eyes of your boss, your colleagues, and your subordinates. All your stakeholders need to say, "He's good at his job"—*you* saying and thinking it is irrelevant.

Become intimate with the work that is needed now in your company and industry, as well as what will be needed in the future from a 360-degree perspective. Get into those types of jobs early on, and stay in!

Find out what the top bosses' biggest goals, objectives, and/or pet projects are. Help them to achieve the results they want. Few bosses will ignore or dismiss someone who is working on a favorite project. Get off projects the big bosses don't like (unless you are 200 percent certain the boss is wrong).

In whatever work you do, provide structure, be a technical heavyweight, possess unquestioned functional skills, work hard, see the big picture, create new systems or processes, step back and see how things could be done better and more cost-effectively, have global smarts, show improvement every year in how you save money and provide growth opportunities, handle the balance sheets, and earn good returns on capital employed.

- If you're in sales, sell more to more people, spending fewer expenses and earning more profit.
- If you're in finance, save your company money and increase revenues and worth.
- If you're in research and development, invent a solution to a problem.
- If you're in information technology (IT), make information more accessible and usable, and do so faster.
- If you're in marketing, creatively and resourcefully get more positive exposure and support sales.
- If you're in human resources, resolve issues, get processes in place, and communicate among all levels more efficiently and effectively.
- If you're in engineering, learn to sell your ideas and get consensus from individuals to get understanding and support before you get in front of the group.

Unfortunately, track record derailers and disqualifiers are many. For example:

- You have technical brilliance, but you are not perceived as an executor.
- You have good ideas, but you don't develop and implement them.
- You are administratively challenged, meaning that things sit longer on your desk than they should; you micromanage too much.
- You don't do enough detail analysis (not nitpicking but detail).
- You need more focus in general.
- You bring more questions than you do answers.
- You miss deadlines and fail to deliver results or deliver the wrong results.

- You grab credit for yourself.
- You don't listen to others' points of view or are arrogant.
- You can't make a decision.
- You partake in stupid office politics.
- And you ignore the advice laid out in this book.

What Does Being Good at Your Job Mean?
What Does It Look Like?

If you choose to be good at your job (because it *is* your choice), you

- Are successful in one of the big areas.
- Think and operate at levels above those expected.
- View the playing field of corporate interests at 100,000 feet.
- Are a strong, inclusive team player.
- Eliminate waste and add value.
- Have a comfort zone interacting at all levels and with all types.
- Are extraordinarily responsive.
- Maintain a positive, energetic, and enthusiastic attitude.
- Have the ability to cut through complex issues; you are good at synthesizing things.
- Bring a new and different perspective; you help people to think differently.
- Do what you say you'll do with high integrity; you're able and trustworthy.
- Present yourself extraordinarily well; you have excellent communication skills.
- Are extremely knowledgeable; you have a global perspective.
- Are outstanding in coaching and feedback; you guide people along.
- Will take a stand but not run over others; you aren't afraid to tackle change in tough issues.
- Ask lots of questions to cause people to think.
- Can envision what will work in the marketplace.
- Think and focus strategically; you minimize minutiae.
- Get the right things done—on time and within budget.

■ Don't say one thing to someone's face and another behind the person's back.

Generate Work for Yourself

In addition to all the preceding, willingly take on harder work than assigned. Look around; see the needs of the business, the department, or the function you're in; and find a gap and fill it. Don't wait to be handed a new assignment. Volunteer for additional duties. Have a self-starter and problem-solver mentality. A favorite thing bosses like to hear is, "I want more work" (along with "We successfully completed that").

If you need to be managed like a new hire and wait until someone brings you a task, you won't be viewed as a high-potential go-getter.

Learn other people's jobs in other departments. Go to another group head and say, "Hi, I'm interested in what you do. If you need help where I can do something on my own time, I'd like to do it." If he or she doesn't take you up on it (which often stems from fear of you taking some of that person's authority), go ahead and follow up with information you've found that would be of interest to the person anyway, such as an article, book, or snippet of information from some connection.

Leaders help others outside their own area. If the person does take you up on your offer, you get a chance to learn, be of service, and get crossover exposure that helps you to evaluate the next direction in which you may want to go.

When you take on additional responsibility, make sure to deliver on it. Not delivering is slightly worse than not stepping up originally. Some simple examples:

> *Early in my career, I joined this company, but I was young and wanted to travel, and my job didn't require it. So I started to volunteer to help recruiting, which got me traveling. The human resources department saw my "free" support of their efforts and rewarded me by asking me to be part of some special events that popped up. I was asked to help at another company occasion on a very short notice but made it happen anyway. That affair had a cocktail party where I met the CEO and got to talking about how I got*

to the event. He asked me to represent him at another corporate gathering outside the organization, where he wanted company representation. And it just kept going on from there.

I act as a clipping service. I scan newspapers and trade publications that will be of interest to my colleagues. I cut them out and send with comments. I don't worry if they've already seen it; it lets them know I've seen it and have taken notice.

I wasn't brilliant, but I was stable and calm and willing to do whatever task needed to be done.

You reinvent yourself when you seek significant responsibility to begin with and then reach for more beyond that, all the while consistently exceeding expectations.

Resist the obvious and easy way. Don't do shortcuts. Don't shirk from the dirty work—"grab a paddle and get wet." Be willing to do something because it's hard, beneath you, and not what you were hired for.

A guy in my company who is definitely on my radar screen uses a certain expression whenever I say, "We need to do some task." He'll immediately respond with a firm, "Consider it done," and about the time I turn around, he is doing something or has already completed it with no fanfare, just action . . . I like that a lot.

Your boss doesn't have the time to give out new assignments. He or she wants someone savvy enough to look around and see priorities in where you should be spending your time. Your discernment shows that you understand the needs of the business and have a finger on the pulse of it, which impresses the boss and makes the white space between you and others bigger.

By generating work, you can be the one who digs a project out of a hole or ingeniously initiates cost reductions in your department.

Don't pressure me for an expanded budget like everyone else is doing; instead, ask for a leaner, tighter budget and see what you can come up with. That will get noticed.

The founder of Cranium Inc., told me the story of having just printed 27,000 copies of the game Cranium in 1998—just after the national toy show was over, where, unbeknownst to him at the time, all new products are introduced and orders made for the next year. Talking with his colleagues in Starbucks about their predicament of having to wait almost a year for the next toy show and paying for the inventory all the while, they looked around and had a life- and career-changing charge. "Let's take our games to where the customers are—Starbucks, Barnes & Noble, and Amazon [places games had never been sold]—not where the games are typically sold [FAO Schwartz, Toys 'R' Us, etc.]."

Work Innovatively and Imaginatively

Take whatever you do to another level. Do what other's won't, don't, can't, or never dreamed of doing. Stretch your thinking and come up with what you thought you could never do—then put it on your "to do" list.

Work at a steady pace that's faster than required and speedier than anyone else.

Get right on the task without waiting to be told, reminded, or nudged.

Don't hang with procrastinators, complainers, or victim-mentality types. Avoid finger-pointing, blaming, complaining (even when others are moaning around you), or putting down coworkers who don't work at the same tempo.

Pray that you get thrust into things you're not sure you can do—and at a younger age than your peers.

Pinpoint problems and opportunities before others. Spot issues before they turn into crises. Think through actions before taking them, and consider the consequences versus blindly, thoughtlessly doing as you are told. In a calm and thoughtful manner, be willing to ask anyone anything to help anticipate and avoid getting the organization into predicaments—even if it's outside your area. Spot possibilities before others propose them.

Handle as many problems as possible by yourself personally. Use your own noggin to solve problems before seeking additional resources or asking for the assistance of others. Enjoy seeing how far your own ability can carry you. Then put that aside and encourage or help others around you to do the same so that they see how their ability can carry them too. Pick up another person's slack when it will benefit the whole.

Produce results that no one can match or that do not permit anyone to fault your performance or doubt or challenge your leadership and ability. Treat small and big tasks with equal importance and results. Complete the work even if others beg off. Despite your advantages in life, your upbringing, and so forth, work like you haven't any. Make sure that every dollar you spend produces more than that dollar in return for the company or it's a waste.

Have the confidence to be willing to be replaced if you can't handle the problems.

Develop People Relationships

If you didn't have the best education or you didn't join the best companies to date, you can still get a collection of the best and brightest mentors, sponsors, and business contacts, friends, and acquaintances.

Regardless of who you are, you need people to help get you through the rocky shoals.

Get your own trusted advisor on the unspoken rules for success.

There's no reason to reinvent the wheel. Learn from others who've gone before you.

Mentors are like having a personal advisory board of directors; experienced and accomplished people who will make time for you when you need it. You can sit and be vulnerable with the person about things you can't discuss with peers, subordinates, or bosses. You can vent about professional progress and office politics, and you can get guidance when you want accelerated learning in market changes, financial issues, staffing, strategy, risk assessment, etc.

Mentors are your sounding board as you make major and challenging decisions, so select ones who are more accomplished, at a higher level, and have gone farther than you. You want ones who've seen more, done more, and are "more than a page ahead of you in the instruction manual." You need at least some of them to have lived through inflationary cycles as well as significant geopolitical events. Whatever age you are you need to get older ones, younger ones, and ones from diverse cultures and the opposite sex too.

Any single individual will not fit all your needs or be available every time you need advice, so you need multiple mentoring friendships. In addition, certain mentors fit for certain times and predicaments.

With the large number of issues you may want to discuss before you act, you "don't want to drain one person dry." Keep in mind that a good mentor has his or her own mentors too, so any single individual might be consumed with his or her own issues when you need him or her for your issues.

> *Everybody talks about having a mentor, but in reality, it happens less than it should. And it's impossible to get to the CEO job without one. I got lucky and had several gentlemen who fine-tuned my maturing process socially, culturally, artistically, and business-wise.*

In some companies, early in your career, mentors are picked for you in an organized program. Use but don't rely on whoever is assigned to you. Getting one assigned to you can be a bit of an unpleasant obligation for that individual unless you prove to be someone he or she really wants to mentor—and would do so with or without the "assignment." The advantage for you in getting one assigned is that it's likely to be someone you normally wouldn't have access to. Obviously, since the company thinks the person merits being a mentor, he or she is certainly worth your fullest use.

A drawback of an internal mentor, especially an "arranged" one, is the potential *candor pitfall*, where the things you discuss get shared internally. Again, this is why you have multiple mentors—inside and outside the company, your town, your industry, your country.

If you wonder why a gifted person would be willing to mentor you, it's because he or she remembers the value he or she received from people along the way and wants to give back and contribute. Smart people know that teaching is also a good way to learn. Accomplished people want to make a difference and feel honored when you care about what they say and think. (If you never ask for help, they don't have that chance to feel good.) Leaders know that mentorship is part of their job.

If the person you ask hesitates, don't take offense; he or she may have limited time, may fear not being available to help, may be looking for his or her own mentor, or in the extreme, may be cautious about any legal exposure.

If the mentor you select agrees, give him or her a brief story about yourself at the start. Don't assume that he or she has your résumé tattooed on his or her forearm; you have to let your mentor know what you're doing, have done, and want to do. One executive had been working in a company over four years, had been promoted twice, but wanted more, so she stopped into her mentor's office and reviewed with him the things she had done and done well. The mentor said, "I didn't know you did all that. You need to be into...I'll help."

Contact the individual's assistant, and check when you can get some time to talk on the phone (you don't have to be face to face). Make it easy for your mentor to help by being considerate of his or her time and schedule. When you speak with the person, clearly but briefly explain the situation you need his or her thoughts on, what you've done, and what you're considering doing. "I have a situation...Here's what I think about it." Then ask what he or she thinks and would recommend.

You want to demonstrate that you've done work on the issue before coming for help.

Listen deeply. Ask questions for clarification. Don't be so in awe of your mentor that you don't push back or question his or her thinking. Consider his or her advice, and decide what to do.

Your obligation to your mentors is to be honest and provide full disclosure. Tell him or her what happened. Tell him or her why you did or didn't follow his or her advice. If you ever have to deliver some bad news to your mentor, do it completely, all at once, and before he or she hears it from someone else.

Follow up and report back; let your mentor know the kind of impact he or she had. Don't let him or her wonder what happened to you.

Share milestones and successes. Compliment your mentor on his or her insight and intelligence.

Give back. Provide your mentor with information of interest or of benefit to him or her, for example, a news piece, magazine article, new book, or support for a cause he or she cares about. An occasional bottle of wine or tickets to a show don't go unnoticed either.

Note that a mentoring relationship is not a place to pitch your product or turn the conversation into a therapy session or a job interview.

You can sustain a single mentoring relationship over a 20-, 30-, or 40-year period (or more)—basically depending on how long you live and when you started it! It's a professional friendship that can be fed like any friendship. Through it all, treat the person like you would want to be treated.

Regardless of where you are in your own career, be a mentor to others. It's required. Help others on their journey; you're not the only person with a dream.

Be a mentor even if you're just beginning your career, both for practice and for reward. Share your knowledge.

I mentor every day, pass on wisdom to help people to anticipate rather than react. It frees people and speeds up their development.

Sponsors, backers, or as some call them, "rabbis" (as opposed to mentors) put your name forward, speak on your behalf, and fight for you in addition to advising and coaching you. You need to "carry their bags" in return, meaning: Be worth sponsoring, have a good track record, be ethical, be optimistic, be good-humored, and be willing to listen and learn. Most important, do unto others as you are lucky enough in having done unto you.

Don't wait until the "luck lightening" strikes you. Find out who the key career influencers are in your organization. Ask your boss, your boss's boss, and human resources (all of whom could be the answer, by the way).

Don't do it quietly in the corner. Be brave, and talk about it.

Your boss is most likely to say, "Don't worry about it; just do your job," which is a valid request. Your boss may or may not be a mentor or a sponsor. He or she is looking for output and hopefully will give you development to help with that job performance. But it is not your boss's role to give you advice in general on career advancement.

Sponsors go further than advising and actually vouch for you. Effective sponsors are in favor in the organization, have insider knowledge, have their own connections, can be objective about you, and have a track record for advancing others. Sometimes assigned mentors can turn into a sponsor for you.

I lobby for certain people who I want my fingerprints on.

I call it a grown-up, Big Brother and Big Sister program.

For example, behind closed doors, "sponsor" Ragesh says, "Juan needs to be in this... job. He's ready." Or "sponsor" Joe says, "I think [your name here] fits the competency model." Chelsea says, "I don't see [your name here] that way." Joe then takes Chelsea for coffee and says, "I'm supporting [your name here] to the next level. How do you feel about it? Will you support my efforts?" Chelsea is likely to say something like, "I'm backing Felix for such and such, so if you agree to support him, I'll assist [your name here]."

Company managers say that promotions don't happen this way, but they do. It's a bonus if a conversation such as this happens for you. But don't wait for it. Sponsors, like human resources, are not responsible for your career.

Sponsors also do more than help you get promoted; they can give you exposure not typically available at your level by putting you on councils or committees or getting you invited to special events or meetings. They let you in on conversations not normally open to you.

Mentors and sponsors are people to get advice from, but at the same time, you have to consider the source, trust your gut, and decide for yourself.

My sponsor and I would have a chat. He'd say, "Do you know so and so is not an admirer of yours?" Then he'd tell me what to do about it.

You have to be the one to seize opportunities to influence those who influence your career.

From old people, seek stories. From young ones, seek technology.

One of my mentors would say, "Sit down kid; let's talk." He was only four years older than me.

You carry out exceptional work when you have a solid track record in the opinion of the constituents involved: (1) You produce the right results because of your specialist skills in a core competency critical to the company, (2) you go beyond what's expected, and (3) you help others do exceptional work beyond what's required. All of this is made possible because of your individual effort, improved by the coaching, mentoring, and guidance from mentors and sponsors

2

You Never Have To Rely on Your Technical Brilliance

- Be able to influence people who don't think like you do.
- Resolve problems—yours and others.
- Delegate effectively.

As a craftsman with a good track record, you must have great skill and expertise in an essential mission-critical core competency. But don't let your talent in that area become a trap, where you get so good at the specialized work competency that you forget to see your business in a holistic way.

Every thing is your thing—yes, you come from a discipline, but you become a generalist. And being a generalist is interchangeable with people skills.

Look for diversity of experiences because to be a CEO, you need to be able to understand and set strategy for every facet of the business.

At the top, you become a generalist among specialists. You make bets on behalf of investors and employees. You pick leaders, override leaders, listen to them, and at some point you're the one who gets to say, "Okay, saddle up."

Empathetically step outside your own work, your own situation, and grasp the interests, objectives, and frustrations of peers, bosses, and subordinates in and out of your specialty. If you figure out how constituents and components play into your and others' successes, you can focus, align, and build effective groups, liaisons, and partnerships beyond your office walls to the industry, the country, and out to the world.

Getting too specialized—too technically brilliant—will limit your upward movement. In fact, it will limit progress totally past a certain level. Instead, you must simultaneously continue getting better in your specialty while you take on generalist skills too. There is no specialist path, alone, to the top, only combined with being a generalist. You will make better decisions, fewer mistakes, and be better able to lead, evaluate, attract, and retain a diverse group (functionally as well as culturally) as a generalist. If you only understand one area (over even two or three), you'll be underdeveloped and unprepared to take on a total leadership role.

You better not be the best of anything except the best at getting your team to do productive things.

The day they made me CEO, I knew I was in trouble. The biggest shock to me was discovering that I had to give up being one of the finance boys. When I was the CFO, I didn't have to treat the sales guy well; as the CEO, I have to treat him well. I could be judgmental of other departments as the CFO, but as the CEO, I had to make them my ally. I went to the different heads and told them I was going to work on their behalf with the rest of the company. Most didn't believe it.

The CEO has 1,000 jobs, and working with his team is just one of them. You're expected to be the visionary and everything else.

⋘◊⋙

I don't do just any one thing. I enjoy making all the parts of the symphony come together.

⋘◊⋙

If you have the reins in hand, all things must matter to you instead of just some things. You simply cannot say, "That's not my thing." It's all-encompassing

Learn, understand, and appreciate others' responsibilities rather than focusing solely on your immediate tasks at hand. Don't mistakenly think that no one else is doing work as important as you. Appreciate how important all parts are and how the whole works. You'll have greater confidence, power, flexibility, and influence when discussing a variety of issues both internally and externally if you do.

If you get a feel for how your work decisions affect profitability and the financial impact of your actions on the entire organization, you're more likely to come up with new ways to increase revenues and profit.

I initiate a series of discussions with each functional head about how dependent he [or she] is on other functions ... marketing with IT, sales with engineering, finance with engineering, sales with IT and finance....

You will be highly valued by management, by human resources, and by executive search consultants the more you have exposure to finance, operations, retail, customer service, marketing, corporate strategy, fundraising, sales, competitors' tactics, and so on.

Even though I'm in banking, I'm a top-level big-picture thinker everywhere I am. For example, when I go to a restaurant, I'm always thinking about where the food came from, how they created the menu and harmonized the food on it, how they coordinated the staff, and what draws the customers.

Know your own job well, but make certain to know other jobs, the marketplace, the business and industry history, the current economic climate, corporate culture, customers, colleagues, senior management, technology, entry/middle management, overall policies, reputation, and the way it all relates together. Get a grasp on how every function in the organization works and the fundamental drivers from top to bottom.

Understand financial impact of your core competency (how your work gets money, makes money, or keeps money). Gain financial literacy in general. Understand financial statements, budgeting and planning, corporate structure, and how equity and debt work—in your organization and in general. (It also doesn't hurt to know compensation, bonus levels, and stock options in your equivalent job with competitors.)

One good outcome of the dot-com bust was that a lot of young CEOs were forced to return to working for a company. Having had generalist responsibility, they became more effective, quicker in specialty roles, because they knew the impact overall.

Because of my generalist experience, at 35 I was running a division with the median age of other decision heads being 54.

I didn't know what the hell I was doing, but I volunteered anyway.

Seek rotation work in other areas, but don't wait until you have a bigger job to grasp who and how things intersect, overlap, and affect each other. Stay on top of things as they change locally, regionally, and globally. Only then can you anticipate, capitalize, and maybe even initiate changes in the marketplace. Upward mobility requires more experience that's general in nature and less functionally specific.

The most transferable skill across functions, companies, industries, cultures, and countries is generalist expertise. Keep up the work in your critical core competency while you grasp knowledge of the big picture. Use both to get known as the best and brightest in predicting needs, and identifying, hiring, placing, promoting, training, developing, managing, motivating, and retaining numbers of talented people.

What Does Being a Generalist Mean?
What Does It Look Like?

If you choose to do this (because it *is* your choice), you

- Take on the concerns of other disciplines.
- Make things better across the board, not just in your specialty.
- Create a consistent high-performance/high-integrity culture and carry that across a wide and diverse audience.
- Affect the entire business in new products, new markets, and new acquisitions.
- Can coordinate relationships with the board, corporate officers, staff, customers, and other constituents, who might include outside partners, suppliers, funders, contract counterparties, local/national/international industry leaders, lobbyists, governance, regulators, industry groups, Wall Street analysts, and the community.
- Ensure that company processes are in place for sound, timely, "no surprise" financial and nonfinancial reporting.
- Comply with legislation and regulatory bodies.
- Attract good employees whom you are willing and able to promote, demote, and dismiss when needed.
- Understand issues, make rational judgments, and draw correct conclusions to solve adverse/complex/wide problems outside your technical expertise.
- Formulate short- and long-term strategies and policies and gain agreement and acceptance of your ideas and approaches.

A generalist goes beyond comprehending all functions but includes the skills of influencing, problem solving, taking "No," saying "No," managing meetings, delegating, and dealing with office politics and bullies.

Be Able to Influence People Who Don't Think Like You or Report to You

Except for gossiping, we spend more time trying to change people's minds than anything else, according to Howard Gardner, Harvard University psychology professor. You will need persuasion skills to get your ideas heard and accepted; recruit and retain people; talk to bosses, customers, colleagues, and peers (and later the media, Wall Street analysts, and the board of directors); and deal with your spouse, children, extended family, and friends.

To persuade, before going into a situation, think about the change you want to make, consider the other person's point of view, take into account the resistance you'll likely receive, gather as much data as you can, and keep all this information in your head (or on paper). Then go talk to the person you need to influence and ask

- What do you want to achieve, retain, and avoid?
- Who, how, when, why, and what will contribute to making a decision?
- What are you willing and able to exchange, give up, barter, or negotiate?

Take what you learned from that person, add it to what you know from other analyses, and then present some options that meet what you both need, want, or expect.

Purposefully influencing is just thought-out conversation. If you make sense to people and you are talking with integrity, people will pay attention and possibly change to your way of thinking. It isn't about hog-tying people to do something they don't want to do. But it does mean being able to find out what they want and how they want it and giving it to them in as close to that manner as possible.

Even if you're the boss and you can just say, "Go do it," you will have only light support, enthusiasm, and improvement from the person bossed. Instead, ask directed questions to get to mutual agreement.

Be prepared to accept the unacceptable response for now, though. Don't be irritated, angry, or turn autocratic. Ratchet up your cooperative effort. Try again later. Time, tenacity, and finesse in your reengaging may turn the person around.

On your own, take the initiative to do a minirotation yourself by doing some ride-alongs with company sales people. It gives them a chance to learn about you and your work, and you to learn about theirs. You develop more connections in and outside the company, appreciate "another world," and broaden your generalist skills.

Resolve Problems — Yours and Others

Be grateful for problems because if there weren't any, you wouldn't be needed. Problems make it fun. This is your job in life and in your work—to overcome obstacles and fix problems. Everything is about overcoming obstacles—every novel, every movie, and every triumph in business or in life.

The fact that you choose to address problems puts you ahead of others who usually choose to ignore and tolerate them or, worse, make them bigger. You get the reputation as the "go to" person when there is a hitch in progress because you won't ignore red flags; accept suspect facts; turn a blind eye to questionable actions and practices; accept overly upbeat news and predictions without testing them out; plead ignorance; blame problems on rogue underlings; or take a deaf, dumb, and blind defense.

Find and define (accurately and well) the right problem to fix as soon as possible. While you are getting "your own house in order," at the same time find out what your boss, boss's boss, or boss's boss's boss has for problems, and try to solve those too.

I found [that] most people want to see their own career move forward, so I'd go off and do something they needed done. Sometimes I got a little bloodied, but I learned.

Offer options. Don't "bring a dead cat without a shovel." You don't have to be the personal problem resolver; there are lots of people to do that. You do have to be the leader who will listen, hear, persuade, and garner support from coworkers to *get* disputes solved. Allow creative conflict. Get the opposing position. Be willing to spend "a period of time at each other's throats."

Stand on your group recommendation. If one out of 10 times your recommendation works, that is better than zero. And if you get two out of 10 times, you've demonstrated 100 percent improvement. It doesn't take 10 out of 10 times. If you make a mistake, correct it. How you handle a setback is watched as closely as the setback. You don't always have to be right, but you do have to act quickly to respond and redo.

When you solve problems, communicate it by telling people what your *group* did to solve the problem. The biggest benefit of solving a problem is that you're free to proceed to the next one.

Be Able to Take "No" and Be Able to Say "No"

First, understand that "No" is the standard answer or response from peers, bosses, and subordinates for reasons of budget, time, to argue an unpopular point of view, to test or challenge you, to be difficult, and sometimes out of laziness. "No" is a complete sentence. It isn't a complete answer. Don't take it as a matter of course if you believe that it could or should be otherwise.

"No" doesn't always mean "No." More often than not it means "Maybe" or "I'm not sure." "Won't" is different from "Can't." Unless you come back and fight for it, your opponents figured they were right.

The word "No" means nothing to me.

Frankly, a quick "No" is better than a long "Maybe" because then you can step back, find a way to reapproach, and change your opponent's mind; even though you may have to jump over hurdles to turn it into a "Yes."

Don't react, but do respond. These are two different things. You can't tuck and run when told "No." Keep asking in a pleasantly assertive manner, with a relaxed smile, and an undisturbed tone of voice, "What if we did this…? What if we did that …? Can you tell me why …?" or almost anything starting with *who, why, how,* or *when.*

Pleasant nagging is sometimes required.

Eventually, a storm of gnats will wear them down.

You might turn the "No" into a "You've been after me four times on this issue. I don't believe it, but go and do it. I may be wrong."

Failing to challenge the "No" is not helping the boss, the team, or the company. Agreeing with the boss is not helping him or her, nor is it grooming you for a bigger job. People respect you more if you bargain harder.

On the other hand, you need to be able to say "No." Give "No" as early as you can so that the other side knows that you'll say it and you give them time to decide their next step. Sometimes say "No" when you'd usually say "Yes" just as a test of the person's convictions. Just as a good boss may say "No" to you to teach you to fight for your position, a benefit of you saying "No" is letting your people learn to fight for theirs too.

Don't say "Yes" too fast. Slow down and weigh your response a little. Don't feel guilty. Don't fall for flattery. When you say "Yes," set boundaries for who, what, when, why, and how you'll do what you committed to.

Stand by your convictions. Say "No" even to your lifeblood. Don't stay on the fence.

The problem with saying "Yes" is that two months later, you have to deal with it. If you really know that your answer is "No," you save a lot of time on both sides if you just say it. Don't delay for two weeks just to make someone feel better.

When you say "No," if possible, offer some suggestions, alternatives, or substitutes: "No, I can't meet you for lunch to talk about the project. We can schedule a half-hour telephone call, though."

Change your mind if you've mistakenly said "Yes." Correct it. Admit that you should have said "No" earlier. Don't feel obligated to explain or defend; you'll only dig a hole for yourself and say more than you need or want. Offer to help the person find a solution at this point so your new response does not unempathetically burden the person. (The pain of you having to go through all these steps at this stage will help to remind you not to so quickly say "Yes" in the future.)

Run an Effective Meeting and Be an Effective Meeting Participant

Most people don't run bad meetings—they run *awful* meetings. Yet, at great expense and time, they continue to have them.

If you can't run an effective meeting, it's better not to have one. The damage you do is multiplied by the number of people there.

Leaders participate in lots of meetings. A vice president alone can have, on average, 70 meetings in a week. Men spend, on average, 11 hours a week in meetings; women spend 8. Of people surveyed by Poly-Vision Corporation, 75 percent said that their meetings could be more effective.

Have fewer meetings and only for very important reasons. Identify a problem, solve a problem, or dispense information to a group simultaneously. Do away with a meeting if the only reason to have it is that it's Monday morning.

Keep the number of people at meetings as small as possible while still including everyone who needs to be there. A meeting becomes more complex with more people.

Focus, and then narrow your focus. Use an agenda to stay on track to deal with the issues. Your job as the meeting leader is to set the agenda, manage disruptive behavior, break deadlocks, do a postmortem, follow up, and plan the next meeting.

Get attendees used to a few simple rules: (1) Deal with difficult issues first (maybe 50 percent presentation, 50 percent discussion), and (2) Don't let someone's pet peeve dominate.

> *I have strict rules for staff meetings, which I will tell people in advance: attendance required, no gossip, no sidebar conversations, stick to the subject, [and] comments limited to three minutes each. Unless someone is expecting a baby, turn off cell phones and BlackBerries.*

Decide who will run the meeting in advance and how others will get feedback from the meeting. Free form may be good for brainstorming, but not for dispensing information.

Physically set up the meeting. Set up the configuration of the room; where various people should sit to enhance the meeting objective.

If the meeting is in the boss's office with the boss behind his or her desk, it will be more intimidating. It might be more effective to go to another person's office, a boardroom, or a totally neutral off-site location (e.g., a restaurant, hotel, etc.).

Consider the time of day when people are there emotionally and intellectually. If you're going to "come down on people," do it at the end of the day so that they can go home and think about it. If you're going to praise them, do it first thing in the morning so that they are in a good mood all day.

Start and end on time.

Seek opportunities to build attendees' self-esteem. You won't get cooperation if you put people down in front of others or put them down period. Use humor. Humor relaxes people and eases candid communication. A serious discussion can be equally effective if an attitude of good cheer is maintained.

And finally, make the meeting quick; don't let it drag on.

Be a good meeting participant too. You're there for one reason, and that is to listen *and* contribute. It's a mistake to just sit there and "take things in." Your involvement can be as simple as a head bob, a "Good point," or a comment like, "Tell me more about . . .," for example, every 15 minutes or so. This doesn't mean that you should interrupt. When you contribute, do it at a moment when you aren't talking over someone else's words or cutting them off. Basic courtesy is noticed.

Contributing does not mean dominating, hogging attention, or grandstanding. When you ask questions, you contribute; when you pontificate, you look silly, waste everyone's time, appear arrogant, and learn nothing.

Don't scrunch and hunch. You will appear bored, tired, lacking in energy, lacking in support, out of it, and not a team player. Sit up straight (it will help your energy), and keep a relaxed expression on your face.

Relax your hands, and sit asymmetrically with your upper body. Don't fiddle, squirm, or play with your pen, coffee cup, etc. Don't touch yourself or pick imaginary or real stuff off your clothes or your body. You come off as totally self-focused, show poor manners, and look disgusting. You want to look controlled versus anxious to be out of there, even if you are anxious to be out of there.

And in a meeting, don't keep a running conversation going on in your mind. Shut it down. Listen to what others are saying without interrupting, finishing their sentences, or guessing what they are going to say.

Don't forget that you are on stage and being watched all the time. Your boss figures that however you handle yourself in a meeting is how you likely will appear in other venues when representing him or her. Your boss wants someone who makes him or her look good.

Again don't be afraid to judiciously joke and kid. You'll improve communication with confident, good-natured humor, look smarter, relax others, set an optimistic tone, and get the same important work done.

Afterwards, memorialize what you garnered from the meeting in a brief e-mail: "This is my understanding. . . ." You keep lines of communication open, minimize misunderstandings, and document in case you end up in court some day.

Delegate Effectively—Before, During, and After the Meeting

When you delegate, you give others an opportunity to do and learn. Open up opportunities for them to shine. Get more done because more are doing it.

A leader either does something personally to get the job done or delegates to get it done. Ask yourself

- What am I doing that doesn't need to be done at all?
- What am I doing that only I can do?
- What am I doing that could be done by somebody else?

  Delegate to the lowest level where the job can effectively be done. Have them report on performance. If they stop reporting, you know the canary died, and there is a problem.

  ⚜

The higher up you go, the less real stuff you do—it's all through people.

Trust them to make a decision, right or wrong. That's the only way to strengthen your whole team.

Always personalize instruction, giving as many orders yourself as possible, or else you undercut your own leadership. Don't use third-party validation, either, such as, "Company policy says that you should...." Always use, "I want you to...."

Add, "Please complete..., approve of..., get back to me by [date and time]."

Assign priorities, and communicate the ranking. Establish intermediary, step-by-step targets to make it easier to attack complex situations.

When you delegate work, hand over the authority too—this is how you develop others. For example, let subordinates conduct meetings or have conversations with key constituents without you being present.

I tell them go ahead and jump. I got your back.

If you don't have understanding and agreement about where you are, you won't get agreement as to where you want to go or when you want to get there. With agreement, you can mobilize what to do. "Here's how we'll get it done." Now, you tell me, "How will you get it done in your area?" Repeat the commitment and priorities weekly, monthly, quarterly, or whenever necessary to create, stabilize, and sustain growth.

Tell your people what you're going to tell them, and then tell them what you told them. Set deadlines. Ask them to confirm that they received all the above. If people don't have a goal, they don't know when they've met the goal, so they don't get to feel good about meeting it.

Hear people out about their reaction to what you told them. They want to be heard. Imagine other people's feelings in the situation. Let them spout off. Be empathetic, but this doesn't mean that you have to agree. You just have to let people feel heard. Mostly people want their positions acknowledged, and mostly they want someone else to make the delegation decision.

Periodically check to see if things are on track.

Don't hint or give innuendo in the hope that people will understand what you want from them. Don't expect them to read your mind or "know better." Tell them what you think and expect from them both early on and straight out.

Take all the blame; share all the credit. Adopt all failures; share all victories.

Tell them; make sure they know what their job is. Give them feed-back. Occasionally do a public execution.

When I have some difficult news to give, I give people a clue about what I'm going to spring on them, give them a few days to get used to it, and then go ahead.

It's very liberating to delegate to other people. It's also scary, because who can you trust? The following CEOs claimed in the business press to have "delegated" and ended up in prison.

You have to rely, you have to trust people. You have to believe. You have to delegate.... I signed off on the information based on what was provided to me and what I was told.
—Richard Scrushy, ex-CEO, HealthSouth

Enron was an enormous corporation. Could I have known everything going on everywhere in the company?
—Ken Lay, ex-CEO, Enron

Bernie Ebbers did not know about the accounting decisions of Scott Sullivan to reassign billions of dollars.
—Reid Weingarten, attorney for Bernie Ebbers, ex-CEO, WorldCom

John Rigas has a right to trust and rely on professionals and his own staff to get the financials right.
—Peter Fleming, attorney for John Rigas, ex-CEO, Adelphia

Despite those horror stories, you still have to get things done through people. You have to trust, have faith, delegate, and empower others. Let them take the reins, but do not allow them to cause you to do your job poorly (like the ones in prison did).

Deal with the Business Bully and Office Politics

First of all, if you have a group of more than one, you will have "politics." Office politics is just human relationships, but with money attached to them—the same human relationships you have among your friends and family. Do not be bothered by the reality of the interdependence and interconnection of organization dynamics. The thing that gives meaning to your work life is the interacting with people and enriching your life because of it.

There are office politics in the astronaut program, on the rodeo circuit, in the priesthood, on charity boards, among nurses at your hospital, at the motor vehicle department, among mail carriers, among mountain men, and among garbage collectors (to name a few).

You can take a positive approach and figure out what the person wants and help them get it or the negative approach, where you disregard the person and tear down their approach.

In any group of people, there is at least one who becomes a bully, which is different from normal politics. You can spot the person who

- Lacks confidence, is insecure, and overcompensates by being a bully.
- Is arrogant, stemming from an out-of-control ego, and therefore becomes a bully.
- Has learned no other way to manage and deal with others than to be a bully.

First, do not fall into any of these categories—or you've missed the point of this book. Second, do not let a bully's behavior hinder you doing your work. Third, do not let a bully's behavior hinder the work of your team. And finally, do not be afraid of bullies; by doing so, you only encourage and empower them.

Nothing will dumb down an organization like someone trying to stir up politics; you've got to fight against a world of B.S.

Deal around, not with, business bullies. Play politics with playing politics.

Business is not a love-in democracy. Not everyone thinks the sun shines out of you—particularly your rivals.

I read what somebody wrote in a company blog about me: "I'd rather have a sister working in a whorehouse than be kin to [CEO's name]." It made me laugh, that's all.

You are being watched from above and below in how you handle the "managerial drive-by shooting," as one put it. When, for example, a coworker takes credit for your ideas, agrees to your face but turns the opposite behind your back, speaks critically about you to others and generally makes your life unpleasant—take the perspective that it's an opportunity to learn, help you grow, pass a test, and make you stronger.

With minor issues, register it, but let it go. Remember, people are seldom out to "get you," but they are out to "protect" themselves, and if you're in the way, you might get stepped on. (You should feel proud that they think you are such a competitive threat that they choose to attack you in this manner.)

Do your homework to understand the facts of the situation. Watch how the person deals with others to check if it's just you or that he or she treats others the same. Talk to the person in private about your grievance. Tell the person what you've seen and heard, let the person give his or her side, and then state what you expect to have happen to clear it up.

Give the person a set amount of time to correct the situation and change his or her ways. If it isn't cleared up per your agreement, there is no alternative: You must deal publicly with the boor and intimidator. In a cool and calm manner, tell the tyrant that your next step is to talk to the boss about the situation. Invite the person to be in on the meeting to tell his or her side. Be honest, clear, and succinct, and keep your sense of humor. Be specific. Nothing kills effective communication faster than general statements such as, "You always..." or "You never...."

If something bugs you, do something about it ASAP instead of sitting and stewing about it.

Address behavior, not character or motive. State facts, and state the consequences and changes needed. If bullying is tolerated in your company, change companies. If it's with subordinates, fire them.

There are no office politics tolerated.... I set an example, and I tell them I'll make an example out of them. There is no game playing and no boundary testing. I had a manager try to take people in a different direction. I demoted him to the lowest level, promoted a subordinate over him, and told him he's going to have to work his way back up.

❧

Bad bosses empower snipers.

❧

View yourself as a global citizen going for international cooperation.

USA Today reports that 51 percent of stress at the office comes from coworkers and 47 percent from the workload. If you cut out the politics, you'd cut your stress in half. Unfortunately, Gallup Poll reports that 17 percent of employees admit being actively engaged in sabotaging the work environment and creating that stress on purpose.

Even with these steps, don't expect to eliminate bullying from happening. Despite how careful you are to live the good and right career path, you will have another encounter with that person or someone like him or her but with a different name. If you think about how many people you work with during the course of a day, a week, a month—15, 50, 500—and if you have one jerk out of the 15, 50, or 500, that's not bad. Still, it's surprising how many people in life seem to think they have a right to give you trouble. The best you can hope for is to minimize the damage they can do to you.

Dr. Leigh Thompson of Northwestern University showed that "bullying bosses beget bullying subordinates; but a top manager with a gentler, compassionate nature begets subordinates who have the gentler, compassionate nature." Don't let bullies get under your skin or into your head. The biggest troublemaker you'll probably have to deal with watches you comb your hair in the mirror every morning.

> *Internal politics and connections can be more relevant and powerful than those found externally. Find time to know people and for them to get to know you. Learn people's strengths and weaknesses in a social environment, and they can be capitalized upon in a working setting. If people can know you in a personal setting, they then will achieve a greater ease to trust you with other information and become closer, more dependent. Build a team of confidents both at the top and within your peer group. Your peer group will grow with you, and they will wield more power and wisdom as you grow older and move up within the company. Spread your wings to other divisions/expertise to have your ideas and name reverberate and to make more people aware of your capabilities and supportive of your positions.*

The only generalist job in the company is the top job. If, at all levels of your climb, you take on generalist skills (interchangeable with people skills), you will be talked about as a high potential candidate for advancement.

3

You Know You Don't Know Enough

- Learn how to improve from what you're learning.
- Take on individual and group learning and hang with good, smart people in and out of the office.
- Seek global awareness.

GATHERING USEFUL KNOWLEDGE FROM MANY SOURCES is one of the most underrated qualities of a leader. Good leaders constantly seek it, collect it, and store it into their brains, computers, or trusted administrative assistants.

I was always in the mode to learn something every day. I'd ask myself, "What's here that would be beneficial to understand?" I read everything I can and tap into everything I can.

You don't have to come into a situation knowing it all. But you do have to come in wanting to learn.

Invest in yourself, in your own education. You can get opportunities, even at your local community college, to be a true global participant.

Without lots of information, you don't have a chance of being a leader. You can't argue your point or even discuss it unless you have tons of facts and material. You can't be a change agent, be globally aware, be innovative and creative, be really good at your job, be decisive, manage your career well, or develop other people.

No investment is guaranteed in life except the investment you make in yourself. Continuously learning is to invest in you. (*Note:* Making an investment in yourself is *not* buying an expensive new car—that's one of the worst investments you can make in yourself. In case you're curious, though, according to an article by Del Jones in *USA Today*, the favorite cars of CEOs are in this order: BMWs, Mercedes-Benzes, Toyotas, and Porsches.)

You learn by reading. You learn from mistakes. You learn from listening and observing. When CEO John Krebbs drives his Mitsubishi 3000 VR4 down Route 28 in northern Nevada, not only does he keep his hands on the wheel at the most efficient 10 and 2 positions but his index and middle fingers are also spread an inch apart. Why? When watching a close-up on television of Emerson Fitipaldi winning the Indianapolis 500, he observed Fitipaldi move his index fingers toward 12 for more controlled steering.

If you feel that you are too old, think you know it all, want to try to skate through, or figure that if you don't know it already, chances are that you're not interested in learning it, you'll limit your advancement.

What you know makes you a lot more than your résumé. You'll be the same five years from now except for the things you learn during those five years.

The best in their field have an attitude of lifelong learning. Warren Buffett says that if you end your day without knowing more than you started, you're not doing something right. Tiger Woods says that he wakes up every day knowing that he can be a better husband, father, and person—as well as a better golfer. The artist Goya at age 82 wrote in a corner of one of his paintings, "I am still learning." My publisher,

McGraw-Hill Professional, has had as its initiative since 2005, "Learn more. Do more."

You don't need to be signed up for an executive MBA program at Harvard, Stanford, or Thunderbird. According to Spencer Stuart, 87 percent of Fortune 300 company CEOs did not attend an Ivy League school. In fact, only 273 of 400 on *Forbes'* 400 wealthiest list have a college degree. Effective leaders want street smarts over school smarts or overeducated and underexperienced.

Walter Kirn, wrote in *Time*:

> *I went to Princeton. There: my résumé. Usually I slip it in more casually. I wait for an opening, a cue, a question. I rarely wait very long, though. As every Ivy League graduate discovers, the greatest benefit of that education is social, not intellectual. I went to Princeton. That statement opens a lot of doors. But should it? . . . I learned instead—and in only a few weeks—that Princeton wasn't heavenly at all but a flawed, all-too-human, institution whose reputation seemed exaggerated compared with the quality of the education it offered. Because I had transferred there from a smaller school—Macalester College in St. Paul, Minnesota—I had a basis for comparison. Although Princeton had far more money and mystique, its reading lists were composed of the same books, and its students were filled with the same questions. But the students carry those books with more aplomb, and they asked their questions with more confidence.*
>
> *That was the Ivy League's X factor. It bred confidence. I remember taking an exam once next to the heir to a legendary fortune who kept peeking at my test sheet. I knew a few things that he didn't, it turned out. . . . Later, many years after I graduated, as I watched my former classmates climb to the top of enormous corporations . . . I felt I was rising with them. I knew deep down, of course, that they, and I, were no better than anyone else, but the world seemed to think we were.*

What Does Being a Learner Mean? What Does It Look Like?

If you choose to do it (because it *is* your choice), you

- Make yourself into what you want.
- Have a teachable spirit.
- Risk asking anyone anything.
- Work to be knowledge-based not opinion-based.
- Have a compulsive curiosity to know all that you can. (Some people question whether curiosity can be taught, and I say that it better be self-taught!)
- Create a culture of innovation and creativity.
- Learn to be a fast, clear thinker.
- Have a good knowledge pedigree.
- Are a student and never stop learning.

Jack Falvey, CEO of Makingthenumbers.com, has had over 36 bylined articles published in the *Wall Street Journal*, has written eight books, was a "careers" cohost on *Good Morning America*, and teaches at University of Massachusetts Boston. He says:

> Life begins when you graduate from college—anything before that is ancient history.... Students getting ready to enter the world of business always ask about how long the training program is. "Forever" is not the answer they are looking for. Those who accept the fact that they have just been appointed director of training for themselves will go further and faster than others.
>
> Learning the fact of the day is just the beginning. Finding out from customers what is going on in the trade so that pieces of the puzzle will begin to fit together is a never-ending project if you are to keep up with an ever-changing big picture. Technology moves. We all must move with it. Where it is going is always a good question to study.

> *You don't have to lead the pack, but it's not a good thing to be deep in the second tier. You have to learn about general business and about world events, not because they will affect your business, but because well-rounded knowledge is apparent to those doing business with you. Trade data, technology developments, and world events are a big part of your training program. These are best learned every day rather than in formal programs. They require time and effort to be fit into a tight schedule. A 10-minute wait for an appointment can translate into two Wall Street Journal articles.*
>
> *You are now attending "graduate school." Study hard; it will pay off!*

Learn How to Improve from What You're Learning

Learning is one thing; getting better from it is another. Conscious, incrementally improved repetition is the key to improved performance. Steps to repeat over and over include

- Pick something you want to get better at.
- Set a goal around it.
- Pick apart what's necessary to reach the goal.
- Part by part, piece by piece, deliberately drill the parts. (Well-done parts make for a well-done whole.)
- On each part, get feedback.
- Seek causes and remedies to problem areas.
- Take that feedback, make changes accordingly, and concentrate on improving at least a little.
- Take the slightly improved, and repeat the effort, feedback, and slight improvement.

Social scientists find that you have to repeat an action 28 times before it becomes a habit. I don't care whether you do it 8, 28, or 228 times, just be sure that each time you are practicing a little bit better execution than the last.

Every task you do, from the most menial to the most significant, can be improved with this conscious preparation: voice-mail messages, report writing, cocktail-party small talk, public speaking, selling, negotiating, and so forth.

I always feel I can do just a little bit better.

Every time you step onto the court, you have to do better. It's like the Olympics.

When you see yourself improving, it becomes interesting. Big changes don't happen overnight, but change can happen from this minute of practice to the next minute, from this day to the next.

Take On Individual and Group Learning and Hang with Good People

Making time to read is not a luxury. Try to do it as voraciously as possible. (And I don't mean your e-mails.) There are only two places where you can read all day without doing much else: school and prison. Since you're in neither, you have to grab what time you can to make sure that you browse something beyond what's required for your job every day.

Listen to (and read) books, and go through local, regional, national, and international magazines and newspapers; blogs; the comics; customer newsletters; your company product brochures; and the World Wide Web — inside *and* outside your areas of interest and specialty. (According to Forbes.com, 51 percent of C-level executives say that their most important source of information is the Web, whereas 22 percent say that it's newspapers.) If you go on Amazon.com, you can buy a subscription to *Skeptic, Free Inquiry, Small Business Technology, African Business, Scientific American, Mental Floss, Reason, Bits & Pieces on Leadership, Management Today, Financial Management, Art Business News, Good Stuff,*

Business Traveler, Biotech Business, Gaming Business, Tennessee Cattle Business, and the *Journal of Applied Christian Leadership,* plus 4,860 other trade and business publications and another 6,000+ nonbusiness publications in the United States alone.

> *I subscribe to customer industry magazines,* IT Journal, CFO Magazine, *and* Human Resources Professional. *Half of it's boring to me, but I do get a different perspective too.*

It is better to read too much than to talk too much. One CEO told me that he had read 40 books about cattle drives to hone his "herding" leadership.

Jump at the chance to go to conferences, workshops, and seminars sponsored by your company, industry association, vendors, chamber of commerce, or local college in your expertise or not. Don't wait to be offered, sent, or required. Study anything you missed in your previous schooling or anything you simply want to know something more about.

Hang with good, smart people, but not just people you know and who are just like you (i.e., accountants with accountants and engineers with engineers). Go out of your way to be around, listen to, and talk with people in the most unrelated function to you and in the most distant industry.

> *I bought a college student's books in classes I missed—paid him twice what he would have gotten otherwise. Heck, he'd even underlined all the important stuff.*

The subject you studied in school doesn't mean anything. What is significant is the training of your brain.

A good target in continuous learning is to simply fill in the gaps of what you've haven't had exposure to. If you studied English, like Michael Eisner of Walt Disney, or premed, like Michael Dell of Dell Computer, or history, like Terry Jones of Travelocity, or law, like John Chamber of Cisco, you could self-study business, engineering, computer science, mathematics, economics, physics, chemistry, finance, accounting, marketing, manufacturing, sales, operations, public speaking, languages, etc. You'll learn something that previously was difficult so that difficult doesn't scare you. You'll learn something useful, whether you actually use it or not. You'll understand how engineers, computer scientists, economists, and mathematicians think—because you'll end up managing them if you're lucky.

Chinese students go to school 230 days a year, U.S. students go 129 days. For every 100 Chinese and Indian students who take advanced math, science, and calculus, there are only 20 U.S students taking the same subjects.

> *When I was young, I worked the midnight to 8 a.m. shift at a garage parking cars. Some of the older workers who couldn't sleep would come and sit and talk. They talked about the war, how they came to America, everything. I learned a lot. Later, at United Technologies, one president head who'd run a couple of companies around the country was a heavy smoker. He'd put in hours in the smoking room. I'd always go in there, even though I didn't smoke, and had hours of one-on-one time with him.*

> *The greatest investment I make in myself is the people I surround myself with. I learn so much; it elevates me.*

> *You get better being around better—from Little League to the board-room.*

> *I look at every situation I'm in to see what I can learn. If I'm visiting people at a neighborhood party, I'll ask questions about everything.*

> *The best schools, the best companies, the best network gets you around the best crowd and therefore the best opportunities. So it's worth the effort to go for the best.*

Pay attention to what's going on around you, capture your observations and ideas in a journal, study your language, vocabulary, and grammar. In other words, prepare yourself for opportunity.

Learn from every encounter, not just business, bosses, mentors, and networking meetings, but also from the bus driver who passes out advice to you on a down day: "It's not the number of times you're knocked down but how many times you get up." Be like the locally famous shoe-shine man in Seattle who listened to customers talk regarding stock trades and built a fortune of his own from what he overheard.

A recruiter of CEOs and boards of directors for technology companies talked to me about developing an attitude of learning from an early age. He reads résumés of potential CEOs every day and hears the "Yea" or "Nay" as names are put on boardroom conference tables across America. He understands what it takes to move up in a career and therefore tries to teach his own 13-year-old son how early decisions in life affect people forever.

He told me that he has been talking with his son about choosing a private high school to attend. Since the son is more interested in computer games than in life work at this point, his father has to initiate thoughtful conversations about long-term career options in a manner that will keep his son's interest. He explained to me:

> My son wanted a cell phone for his birthday, so I said I'd get it for him with a few conditions. He'd get the phone that he wanted if he'd agree to (1) read 250 pages a month from a book of my choosing and (2) every day read one article from the Wall Street Journal *to discuss later.*
>
> Although I've personally had a great deal of career and financial success, I know I haven't done all that I could or maybe should, and I see that pattern of unrealized potential in my son. So I want him to grasp the importance of today's decisions and their impact down the road.
>
> Since he likes video games, I have him look at who made the hardware and software that he's using. I ask him to tell me why he likes it, why other kids do, and why he thinks it's successful. And I have him Google the company and read about its history.

I suggest that he look at its stock, follow it a few weeks, read articles about the company history or new-product development, and anything else he can look up. In some cases, I buy a couple of shares of stock for him to watch. I listen to Jim Cramer, who says, "Instead of buying five DVDs from Disney, buy one share of stock."

I want him to have intellectual stimulation in whatever he is doing. We had a three-hour conversation about this last week, and he actually stayed tuned-in with me, which is amazing since communication among kids is so superficial nowadays. They don't even talk to other kids; they just text each other.

I explained that each article he reads, for instance, is like one dot of information and that one dot may not mean much on its own, but if you collect 100 or 1,000 dots—points of information—patterns and cycles start to form. And I tried to explain that understanding of cycles will give him a belly full of instincts and insights years ahead of what others have. See, I want my son to have experience not just one way—say when markets are cresting—I want him to understand a bad market too. By seeing the dots, I'm hoping he'll learn to anticipate when things will turn bad and what might turn it around. Every four to five years a new bubble ends, . . . you need to weather times . . . know that what's relevant now is seldom relevant five years from now . . . eras come and go. It's like a general going off to war. You don't want one whose only experience has been in peace time. You want one who's been in war as well as peace time to have experience in pattern recognition of what might happen next.

I also occasionally go over résumés that are particularly interesting with him. I showed him one from a man we'd placed into a top job. He'd graduated from Brown, joined McKinsey & Company, got a Wharton MBA, and joined Disney. Since my son likes most anything Disney, it perked his interest. The candidate got the opportunity to work alongside the company CEO, and now, within 10 years, he's being put into a top job.

I tell him you've got to work hard, and then you'll get lucky. And I want my son to understand all this before he enters high school.

Seek Global Awareness

If you do not go out into the whole world literally and figuratively, you will look ignorant, be ill-informed, and be unprepared when the world comes to you (which it will) in the form of customers, vendors, peers, and bosses. A good thing to learn is global awareness. You get a fresh perspective, are more open minded, are less prejudicial about race/culture, and you think more broadly.

> *People in the United States don't even know what time our work day starts or ends or when we take lunch here in Hong Kong. It's like we are working on Mars.*

> *When you take your next flight to grandmother's house, consider that the Boeing 787 Dreamliner plane you're on has wings from Japan, wingtips from South Korea, a horizontal stabilizer from Italy, an engine from Britain, a cargo door from Sweden, landing gear from France, and a movable trailing wing edge from Australia.*

> *I go to bars in New York. They are filled with people from all over the world. You get a broad world picture. One person is a filmmaker from Finland, another is a cab driver from Russia, and another is scouting locations in the south of France for putting in an Abercrombie and Fitch store.*

To constantly seek information outside your "world":

- Ask for a foreign assignment.
- Interview with foreign-owned organizations to increase your chance for an international assignment or stint.
- On your own, study *global* macroeconomics, finance, strategy, organization and structure, marketing and brand management, sales, and human resources management.
- Stay current with world news; most cable companies have international feeds. (Instead of just checking your local weather,

check on Tanzania today too.) At this writing, some of the shows you can TIVO include *India Business Week, Worldwide Exchange, Business Arabia, Business Russia, European Closing Bell, European Power Lunch, World Business, Managing China, Managing Asia, Bloomberg Asia, Business China, Business Pakistan, Business Australia, Europe Market Countdown, Asia Squawk Box, Squawk Australia,* and *Squawk Europe.*

- Recruit a diverse team, including first-generation coworkers available from around 89 different countries.
- Learn a second or third language. (One CEO tells me that he is fluent in Spanish and Scandinavian—quite a combination—and can ask "Where is a good restaurant?" in six other languages.)
- Request a bilingual administrative assistant.
- Take classes at an international business school.
- Read annual reports from foreign companies.
- Look inward at your own company (even though you work in domestic operations), where there could be partnerships, divisions, or subgroups with global involvement. For example, Anheuser-Busch owned Crown Beers India before it was bought by InBev from Belgium; Tyson owned the Indian poultry producer Godrej; Heinz owns French sauce and salad dressing maker Benedicta; Smithfield Food owns Chinese and European businesses; Kellogg owns assets of a Chinese cookie and cracker company; Alberto-Culver owns the Swedish company Cederroth.
- Vacation outside the United States, and not just Cancun! Dream about signing up for Richard Branson's SpaceShipTwo to blast into space (precise availability dates are still up in the air) or go to Laos or Vietnam, safari in Botswana, bike in rural Argentina, visit Masai villages, do a dig in Greece, cruise the Galapagos Islands, trek on Mont Blanc, or paddle the Mediterranean waters off Crete—but get required vaccinations per government recommendations first!
- If the budget doesn't allow for such travel, read letters and diaries of early travelers such as Emily Eden or Marco Polo;

visit Google Earth, or at least subscribe to *American Express Departures* magazine.

If you're a minority, understand the majority. If you're a majority, understand the minority.

I don't want one of those employees where everything he knows about the world he read in the local paper and saw on CNN. If his world is his house, he's not for me.

A recount of one CEO's international reminisces:

> While based in Argentina, I kept physically sharp and fit by learning Latin dance and drinking red wine, which kept me in a positive mind-set, and as a result, the company I managed had a positive outcome.
>
> In Nigeria, I learned African dancing, interacting with 500 tribal people, resulting in a positive mind-set that helped in long-term financial decisions that affected the oil market with the United States—that and playing golf with international leaders. My life changed forever in Brazil, where I stopped watching television or surfing the Web. They call it the devil's curse there.

As much as you know—and I'm sure it's a lot—gather more and more and more information. You don't have to memorize a Greek tragedy, but you can garner one point here, another one there, and another—and all of a sudden you have a chunk of information that no one else has— information not garnered from the usual sources.

4

You Have Fire in Your Belly

- Set your goal.
- Gut it out. Try hard. Try hard again. Try harder.
- Avoid pessimistic people.

IT'S NOT A DEGREE ON YOUR WALL OR TITLE ON YOUR RÉSUMÉ, it's your attitudinal aura of choice. Life is difficult. Work can be a pain. Family, friends, and coworkers will disappoint you. There is a lot of sadness in the world. It's your choice to succumb and give in to "futilitarianism" or not. *Choose not to.* Despite everything pushing you to succumb, just don't. Stubbornly refuse. Be different—be hopeful, rosy, even buoyant—just for the fun of it. It's totally an option. As with integrity, to have it, you don't have to have been born in the right family, gone to the best schools, or worked for the best company. It's a choice you make today and remake every day you live.

There is *one* step to acquiring a more optimistic, passionate, enthusiastic, energy-for-life point of view. That one step is to *choose your perspective on things*. Persistently take on a productive, constructive view toward things instead of a destructive angle. Your ability to be happy is in direct proportion to your ability to rationalize.

> *Every morning I awake and I walk onto the stage of life and choose whether it will be a comedy or a tragedy.*

It's not absolutely necessary to be a happy, optimistic person all the time—but it helps. Regardless of what attitudinal environment you were raised in, what your tendency is, or what people around you are, you can choose to be an optimist. Train yourself to choose an optimistic point of view about everything despite the actuality. Your reality can be based entirely on your chosen perspective, and it will be as good a "reality" as anyone else's. Whichever thoughts you tend to carry around in your mind tend to prove you're right. A positive perspective *might* get you somewhere; a negative one will get you nowhere.

The only control you need more of in life is control over yourself. The smallest attitude adjustment can change around your whole world. Your brain and every cell in your body listens and corresponds to what you tell it.

> *"I don't believe in failure" is my mantra.*

One CEO and avid art collector said to me, "The good thing about my wife leaving me and taking all the art in the split is that it gives me an excuse to buy more."

You can complain about getting older or be glad you've lived long enough to be old. You can count your blessings or add up your problems. You can say you're having "hot flashes" or a "power surge." (I suppose that you can say that you gave a "strategic deception" instead of a "lie"— following our discussion on integrity!)

Again, I know there is plenty to be unhappy about in your life—war, global hunger, illness, loneliness, aging, death. Still, as depressing as it is, and no matter how bad it is, it's worse elsewhere.

If you count your really, really bad days, what do you get, five or six in a year? Not that bad out of 365. (What's "bad," by the way? You have an office mate who doesn't smile back when you say hello and you think he talks about you behind your back? That's nothing compared to a cowboy I know who saddles up with a broken shoulder, six busted ribs, and a sprained ankle and rides out in the dark in 28 degree weather with the snow blowing sideways to find a lost calf so that it won't die. Then he gets up the next morning at daybreak to find another strangler, but with some frostbite on his fingers from the night before. And he considers himself one of the luckiest people alive.)

"Ambition" as I write it is not the negative definition of ambition: manipulative, unsavory, self-advancement, self-aggrandizement, or self-adulation.

The work you do. If it truly matters—it becomes a part of you. Like the mechanic who never really loses the oil stains under his fingernails, our work stays with us wherever we go.

When I was very young, my father told me, "If you can't get up and look forward to going to your job every morning, you're in the wrong job." If you don't think about it as work and a 12-hour day goes by quickly, then that's your passion.

Jim Holt wrote on the work of British psychologist Richard P. Bentall for the *New York Times.* "There is consistent evidence that happy people overestimate their control over environmental events, give unrealistically positive evaluations of their own achievements, and believe that others share their unrealistic opinions about themselves and show a general lack of evenhandedness when comparing themselves to others.... Indeed, Bentall has proposed that happiness be classified as a psychiatric disorder." Okay, note that Bentall is both British and a psychologist— some would say neither is exactly known for being jovial or joyful.

Economists David Blanchflower of Dartmouth College and Andrew Oswald of Warwick University in England studied a person's satisfaction in life. From their research, they concluded that going from having sex once a month to having it at least weekly is roughly equivalent to the amount of happiness that an extra $50,000 of income would bring to the average American. (Okay, so this Brit isn't that bad.)

Other studies conclude that if you make over $100,000 a year, you're slightly happier than those making less. (Duh, right?) Another study determined that Fortune 500 CEOs are slightly happier than their private company counterparts. Another study of 44 countries indicated that Americans are the most optimistic people, thinking that they can exert some control over circumstances around them, and the Chinese are the least optimistic.

American Psychological Association research shows that moderately happy people earn more money, live longer, have more friends, and do better work. Worldwide studies find that additional benefits include

- Better physical health (less cardiovascular disease, pulmonary disease, diabetes, hypertension, and upper respiratory disease)— according to the National Academy of Sciences
- Less depression
- Less mental illness
- A sense of community
- A feeling life has a purpose

At least one of these benefits has got to appeal to you and cause you to embrace this attitude for the benefit of your team, your family, and yourself. Regardless of any of these benefits, I am talking about you—you and me, actually—and what we can and need to do each minute of every day.

If, instead, you choose to give up and give in, you will fail yourself. Success requires sustained, optimistic ambition. Don't let setbacks hit you harder because you've set high expectations for yourself. Too many people start out like a Roman candle in their careers, full of ambition, energy, and enthusiasm, and then a baby, a large mortgage, a second car payment, or an unsatisfying job—a loss of confidence—causes a fear of losing any of the preceding and results in a midcourse slowdown, a fizzle, and a stop altogether.

Sadly, around 35 to 40 years of age, the dogged hunger to make a difference and make a mark wanes and fades.

It's never over until you stop trying. No one can do everything needed "by the book," but nearly everyone can do more than they think they can.

One manager told me that he tries to do the good things at the right time. My thinking is, How would you even know which is the right time?

They all are. You can't reserve this for the right time, right people, or right situation. To be ready when necessary, you have to be ready when not necessary.

Drive is more important than intelligence.

If you're lucky enough to have passion for what you do, you're lucky enough.

The number one criterion that I want in an employee is to be unrelentingly positive. Someone who will always find good answers; always find good compromises. Don't tell me there are problems. I know that. Tell me, "Here are the solutions."

Your eyes are focused on the prize. The thought of your goal is always in the background. If you have an extra half hour, you do something productive toward it. You prepare yourself all the time.

What Does Optimistic Ambition Mean? What Does It Look Like?

If you choose to have it (because it *is* your choice), you

- Know what you want to do before someone knows it for you.
- Are committed to worthwhile accomplishment.
- Like and enjoy your job.
- Have happy energy combined with intellectual motivation.
- Do what you have to do to be able to do what you want to do.
- Have the kind of attitude that is good for people who hire you, good for people who work with you, good for people who follow you, and good for you.

- Drive results in the economy, the country, and the world.
- Enjoy a cocktail of sustained passion, energy, and infectious enthusiasm—and you understand the following story.

On his sixth birthday, Jerry, a CEO friend of mine, found alongside his birthday cake eight college brochures that his mother had collected for him. "Here, you need to choose one," she said. "It's your choice." Jerry picked up and carefully looked at each brochure one at a time. He could read a lot of the words because his mother had home schooled him prior to kindergarten. Notre Dame's brochure had the most eye-catching photos with lots of trees and a lake (something he didn't have in the high-desert part of Utah where he and his mother lived alone and relatively poor). "This one," said Jerry.

"Good," she smiled. "Now make a wish, blow out your candles, and open your presents."

Jerry explained to me years later that his mother's actions were not to force him into something he didn't want to do. Rather, discussion about his education was as much a part of daily life as brushing his teeth, doing morning chores, and finishing his schoolwork. It was the world he was brought into, like a golfing parent might introduce golf to his or her child or the son of a football coach might become a player. Jerry saw it as a child and later as an adult: His mother's belief was that a good education from a name university would give him a better life. Jerry was on board with that goal even before the age of six.

The summer before going into ninth grade, in between his lawn maintenance jobs, Jerry sent away for Notre Dame's student application form—three years before he would actually use it. When he received the application, he spent the next few weeks studying the requirements he would need: course work completed, test scores, a personal essay, letters of recommendation, extracurricular activities (e.g., sports, clubs, yearbook, newspaper, student government, etc.), community involvement, and jobs outside of school.

With this blueprint of what would be used three years later to determine his acceptance into Notre Dame, he began laying out his plan of activity for high school. Every decision was made with consideration of how it fit into the total picture of a stellar university application that he saw as a tested template of what it took to be successful to get in.

Set Your Goal

Make a list of what it will likely take to achieve your goal, and rank the list in order of priority. When you are derailed, rejected, or sidetracked, go back to your list to get refocused.

Big goals happen from daily effort. You need to always have the future target you are going for tied to something you are currently doing to get there. Start, continue, and complete steps toward the goal.

Nothing will overwhelm your fear and procrastination like the excitement that comes from having something you thought of and planned out come through. You'll wonder why you haven't done it sooner and more often!

> Radio and talk show host Tavis Smiley writes:
>
> *The tragedy of life does not lie in not reaching your goal. The tragedy lies in having no goal to reach. It is not a calamity to die with dreams unfulfilled, but it is a calamity not to dream. It is not a disaster to not be able to capture your ideals, but it is a disaster to have no ideals to capture. It is not a disgrace to not be able to reach all the stars, but it is a disgrace to have no stars to reach for.*

Any individual who decided to write a letter to the editor, write a book, take on a more complex job, initiate a job move, change employers, or even run for president of the United States did the same things: set a goal, took a piece of it, and then started, continued, and completed.

My goal was always to have a day where I wasn't sure of the outcome.

Gut It Out. Try Hard. Try Hard Again. Try Harder

When you wake up, seize the day or the moment, and repeat that tomorrow. Your chosen attitude and action maintain, stabilize, and make sustainable your ambition. There is no secret other than *don't give up, keep plugging, and endure when you've got trouble or inconvenience.* (For a 12-round fight, professional boxers throw, on average, 140 punches. Antionio Magarito threw a record 1,675 punches in one 12-round fight— that's try, try harder. Even more impressive is the man in his thirties who is deaf, blind, mute, and quadriplegic yet has two children's books published, and his stage play is in rehearsal.)

Just don't stop. Do it to the point of gagging.

If someone closes a door, jump through a window.

I'm tenacious. Anything relatively important in life requires nagging yourself on. Now, my son, he's willing to work just as hard—but not during surfing season.

Experts say that 70 percent of energy comes from feeling "up," hopeful, positive, engaged, and focused. Rest, diet, exercise, and health make up only 30 percent.

The people who don't make it give up somewhere along the way. It isn't that they didn't have what it takes. They and you have to hang tough and not let complacency set it. For most people, work is hard enough without pushing harder, so they don't. If it all was totally easy, everyone would do it. As the sign reads in Mac Cook's construction office, "Many people take aim, but few pull the trigger."

They said "Give up," that it couldn't be done and that I'd regret it. They were wrong.

Avoid Pessimistic People

You will hit inevitable bumps in the road without help from others. Other people, the media, your personal life, and the world in general all can bring you down if you let it.

There are people who have no interest in being happy or optimistic. Their negative, self-defeating attitude feeds and grows like bacteria in a Petri dish. Some people erroneously think that being gloomy and glum shows a critical and analytical assessment of things. Steer clear of them. Despair is fine for a poet, but not for a leader. Don't be guilty or embarrassed about being generally upbeat—you need to be if you're going to lead others.

Grouches pull you down; cheerful people pull you up.

At first, my people thought I was Pollyanaish because even when unpredictable things appear, I tend to think it will work out. I paint a positive picture. The glass will never be full, but it is at least half-full or more so and is getting filled even more.... Things can get bumpy. Time takes care of it. If you don't get rattled, most things pass.

Shirley Ann Jackson, president of Rensselaer Polytechnic Institute at the University of Rochester, spoke at a graduation ceremony: "I am an optimist. I am short, and short people can only see the glass as half-full. So optimize who you are and what you are. Optimize your experiences and what you have learned. Optimize others. Optimize your opportunities. Seize them and do meaningful things."

Work is not to produce; it's to give value to life.... when I go to work, I tell my wife, "I'm off to the games." That's how I view business. It's fun, like playing games when I was a boy. You experience winning, losing, cheaters, gamesmanship, psychological ploys—and most important, not to take things personally. Even business trips are like the excitement of going on a field trip in school. Remember how thrilling it was? That's how I view what I do every day.

If you went to work at Berkshire Hathaway, optimistic ambition is required, that is, if you want to keep up with Warren Buffett, who says that he "tap-dances" to work every morning.

Fire in your belly sustains your ambition when you are around negative people, experiencing setbacks and disappointments, recovering from mistakes, and getting feedback. It also inspires and motivates other people to start a little fire in their bellies too.

5

You Feel Broadly Adequate

- Bolster your self-confidence with self-assessment.
- Expect acceptance; you're adequate.
- To get more confidence, do confidence-building things.

CONFIDENCE IS THE DRIVER BEHIND EVERYTHING IN THIS BOOK. People are drawn to you; they want to be around you, do like you, learn from you, and be highly thought of by you. People are happy to follow you because you are more fun to be around.

> *If there are ten traits to becoming a leader, the first seven—no the first eight—would be confidence.*

> *I would rather have a confident individual than merely a smart or competent one. An "A" student is fine and good, but not good enough.*

> *Overconfident ones beat underconfident any day.*

With confidence, you hire and develop the right people because you aren't jealous of the abilities of others. You aren't afraid to surround yourself with people who are better than you. Fewer slackers, dingdongs, and knuckleheads slip through your recruiting process.

There is an absence of trepidation among your group because neither you nor they—by your example—feel vulnerable in being wrong. Differing opinions get voiced because folks aren't apprehensive of your insecurities. Time and effort are not wasted in irrelevant and insignificant thought or activity.

Confidence is a game played between your own two ears.

It took me several years to realize people saw me and my accomplishments, not the poor, abused girl with alcoholic parents. I spent a lot of time in that ineffective mind-set.

You'll make decisions sooner because advancement, not fear of failure, is the driving force behind your actions. Your and your people's delegation improves because you don't fear mistakes or cause fear in your people. More things get accomplished. You get a motivated, energized workplace instead of one drained by timidity and feelings of inadequacy.

Feedback is not viewed as an attack on your character. Interdepartmental politics are minimized in your presence because you aren't threatened by people.

Communication improves because you don't feel compelled to show how smart you are, preferring to listen and hear how smart others are.

When you represent your team and company, you both fit in with what's expected from a leader and stand out from the populace.

In a public company, if the Street doesn't believe you're confident, your stock gets dinged that day.

Important note: The confidence that I write about is *not* that of the Washington lobbyist who wrote in his advice book: "Confidence = white shirt + tan face."

What Does Confident Look Like?

If you choose to have it (because it *is* your choice), you

- Are comfortable in your own skin.
- Handle whatever hits you no matter how many pressures.
- Have an ego that is "in check"; you haven't an ounce of conceit.
- Feel neither self-conscious nor superior.
- Exude lots of emotional strength.
- Fail to act embarrassed with what people think about you and shrug off attempts at insults.
- Freely admit imperfection and ignorance in many areas; you listen for better ideas.
- Credit luck with many of your achievements.
- Look at your own strengths and weaknesses with utter detachment; sometimes you volunteer your own limitations and always admit your mistakes and missteps.
- Have pride but don't act too proud.
- Feel relevant, never irrelevant.
- Have a sureness of your powers to get a job done even with the unknown, complex, or inexplicable.
- Hold no delusion about yourself; you can look at yourself objectively and laugh at yourself wholeheartedly.
- Shut up before you berate, bad mouth, or insult.
- Can say "No" without explanation and can take "No" without affront.
- Feel comfortable being uncomfortable.
- Don't need approval.
- Are complimentary toward others instead of skeptical and jealous.
- Seek out the smartest person in the room instead of acting like the smartest person in the room.
- Think of yourself less often instead of thinking less of yourself.
- Free up your mind with peace of mind even when relinquishing control.

- Respect others.
- Put people around you at ease regardless of how you feel yourself.
- Are talked about by others as sure of yourself, cool, self-reliant, self-possessed, well-balanced, self-controlled, poised, self-assured, and sangfroid.

I had that personal confidence early, from my parents, sports, and my schooling at Rice University as an engineer. One of my first bosses told me years later that he'd hired me because in the job interview, while I was sitting slightly slouched, with one leg over the arm of the chair, I disassembled, repaired, and reassembled my cigarette lighter while answering his questions. I looked like a confident person to him and that's what he wanted.

You, I, and everyone else has insecurities; the only difference is in our ability to camouflage them. The choosing is yours.

Regardless of whether you're short or tall, black or white, everything comes down to controlling your own brain—those eight pounds of meat in your skull. You cannot be a leader in your life if you cannot command your own mind. No one has control over you like you do. If you abdicate that self-control, you're the one who will suffer, as will your family and coworkers.

We're all one point away from insecurity. You have to camouflage your less-than-confident feelings.

It goes in waves depending on what's going on.

I'm always afraid. The earth is shaking as I walk down the hallway. I've been scared the last 10 years. But I don't succumb to it. I can't succumb.

Self-doubt is my demon; I have my dark moments. . . . I carry a little card around with me; it's sort of my prayer. It reads, "Fear Nothing."

I worry that I'm fooling everybody as I try to hide the insecure jerk and half-performing idiot that I sometimes feel I am.

Bolster Your Self-confidence with Self-assessment

To bolster your confidence at this moment, do some honest self-attitude assessment of where you are now. In other words, appreciate your current status. Think about what you're especially good at now and what you have going on for yourself. Everybody has a lot more than they think about on a regular basis. What's painfully obvious to you is a blazing revelation to someone else. Write every ability that you're proud of about yourself: car mechanics, computer games, writing reports, public speaking, teaching, following advice, getting respect from your peers, saving money, drawing, clipping coupons, cooking, children rearing, dog training, drawing caricatures, singing, cleaning up messes, identifying bird species, gardening, telling a story to illustrate a point, constructing an e-mail, debating a position, holding to your convictions, keeping your word, telling the truth, good posture, self-disciplined, organized, persistent, easy to talk to, deal well one on one, good phone voice, good grammar, good taste, good judgment, good intuition, able to multitask successfully, effective, technically brilliant, hard worker, and dependable. Seriously, jot down your list right now. Do it in the margin of this book (unless it's from the library), and write small so that you can get a lot on the page. Keep adding to it as more thoughts come to mind.

Review your life and how (given what you were given) you have a pretty respectable, if not stellar, education, have gotten jobs in suitable as well as excellent companies, and have done good, if not spectacular, work in situations you've been in.

Bring to mind past positive feedback, compliments, and anything else you take pride in.

Add other things about you, such as good parents/family/friends around you, being in relatively good physical shape and good health, and being lucky enough to have been born in a free country—or immigrated to a free country.

Just thinking about what you have, where you've been, and what you've accomplished has to add to your self-esteem a little at least. Don't take those things for granted.

I don't need a high-profile life or the trappings—the stuff. This is not my identity. If my name is never in the Wall Street Journal, *I'm okay with that. I know what I can do.*

Too many times in self-development endeavors it's all about what you need to do more of, do differently, or do better. You forget to weigh in on all that you already have going for yourself. For most of us, given what we've been given, we've done pretty well.

What you bring to the table—who you are and what you can do—is a sufficient starting point. If in your self-examination you see a gap—"Hmmm, I'm about 10 pounds overweight" or "I need more accounting acumen"—do something about it. You will gain confidence in (1) knowing more about yourself, (2) realizing that pointing out a deficiency beats someone else doing it (with this self-knowledge, you can chose to do something about it), (3) understanding that choosing to make a change puts you in control and not under someone else's control, and (4) knowing that you're empowered.

Expect Acceptance; You're Adequate

While all those things that you're good at are fresh in your memory, appreciate the fact that you are broadly adequate. I know that this doesn't seem grand and great enough to many of you, but if you think about it, the flip side of being adequate is being inadequate, which is what people who lack confidence feel. You can go for grand and great if you insist, but for a start, target being adequate—no, broadly adequate! That is sufficient. Right now, you are a human being who is able, ample, sufficient, and plenty capable enough.

Tell yourself, "I'm adequate as a parent, spouse, boss, friend, peer, mentor, coach, sibling, leader" and the rest. (Go ahead and say it to yourself right now, preferably out loud. See how realistic it sounds to you—because you speak the truth.)

Hug yourself every once in a while.

Expect acceptance from the general public as a broadly adequate individual. This is all that confident people do. Valid imagination in managing where you want to be and how you want people to see you is more important than any supposed reality to the contrary.

> *We spend most of our lives being afraid of other people or of how we are perceived by other people. I wish I had realized sooner that other people spend most of their time being afraid of me or of how I perceive them.*

On average, you have 50,000 thoughts a day. It takes intense concentration and persistence to manage them. Thomas Crook, president of Psychologix, discovered that after 35 years of age, on average, we lose 1 percent of our brain volume a year (and that doesn't account for the lost brain cells from extracurricular activities!). Better make sure that the part that remains is well managed and that attitude atrophy doesn't set in as well—so tell your brain what it needs to be told.

When self-doubt, fear, anxiety, hesitation, trepidation, and dread slip in (or get pounded in), go back to your list and strong mind-set that you are equal, able, qualified, trained, and sufficient to manage whatever you're in—as much as most anyone else. You're broadly adequate.

People look at you and see what you think of yourself (which is based on what you tell yourself), and they treat you accordingly. We *know* this, but still we give ourselves too much substance abuse of negative self-talk, putting toxic waste feelings of being unfit, incapable, or incompetent in our brains. Stop it!

> *The big differentiation is the midlevel person who really believes he is in control of his destiny. It comes across in how he will speak to me. He'll say, "Here's a problem, and here are the two or three things I'm going to do to mitigate it." . . . Five percent who work for me are solution-oriented; 95 percent seek direction, support, and affirmation.*

You are your first opponent in life. Well-intentioned training, schooling, and socializing from bosses, teachers, and parents often result in feelings of inadequacy. Squelch that. Feed your brain what you want it to believe (which certainly makes more sense than reinforcing what you don't want it to accept, doesn't it?).

Buckminster Fuller wrote, "Everyone is born a genius; the process of living de-geniuses you."

When you elect feeling broadly adequate, you will experience a tsunami of self-esteem. If you don't make that choice, you will be like a cork in the ocean—every wave of challenge, attack, criticism, and setback will bounce, bob, roll, and knock you around.

In every action you take or decision you make, do it from a perspective of feeling adequate—not inadequate—regardless of your status or standing. It's your choice. *You* decide that you're "not enough" or that you are.

You always have to think you're right strongly enough. It's true; I believe there is no chance I will not succeed.

To Get More Confidence, Do Confidence-Building Things

Act brave; it's not required to be brave. Do something scary that you haven't done before (and I don't mean parachute off the Eiffel Tower).

Preparation increases confidence, we all can agree. Therefore, an example of a brave, confidence-building decision would be to take action before you have all the time and resources to be totally prepared. Ask yourself, "What's the worst thing that could happen?" And if it's tolerable, do it now, not later.

Decide to act self-assured regardless of how you actually are. Don't wait until you *feel* it; it may never happen. To change, change. The change will follow.

As you behave, you will eventually feel. People take you as you present yourself. But you have to keep at it to see results.

You improve by incremental improvements after feedback. Whatever you chose to do, be braver, stretch, reach, and go farther than you have in past encounters and activities.

Surprise everyone — including yourself — by doing something more daring or nervy this afternoon over what you did this morning. Then this evening, boldly top that. Tomorrow morning, venture beyond that. Tomorrow noon, dare beyond that. Tomorrow evening, fearlessly go farther.

It can be steps as simple as talking to your boss in a clear, firm, unwavering manner versus vacillatingly wishy-washy. It might mean engaging in conversation with a stranger. It could be making a decision with only 6 solid facts instead of the 26 that you're more comfortable with.

You get the point: *To gain confidence, do confidence-building things.* You'll surprise everyone, including yourself, as to what you can do. And really, what do you have to lose?

Frankly, I hope you do have something to lose. I hope that you get into a sink-or-swim situation. Because if you survive it, you will learn the lesson in my friend's teenage daughter's new tattoo, "If it doesn't kill you, it makes you strong."

> *The stock market crash of 1987 was a crisis for my company. I was in my early thirties and called on to do three and four press briefings a day. I had to perform or not. Your confidence grows when you're called on to rise to the occasion in a crisis.*

> *Life is the biggest challenge to confidence.*

> *Confidence is a decision, not a state of being.*

Your *will* is as strong as or stronger than your *skill*. Or, as the late comedian George Carlin put it, "People with low self-esteem deserve it."

Having an "ego the size of Grand Central Station" could be used to describe the European leader who arrived late for his audience with the Pope and then reportedly sent a text message during the meeting. He (you and I) needs to keep his (our) ego(s) in check to be a leader.

A superiority complex, ego out of control, egomania, arrogance, and swagger of success all ding your drive toward leadership. This is behavior that is widely understood as overcompensating for personal insecurities.

Everyone needs some feeding of their ego, but if yours is insatiable, you're not a leader.

You derail confidence others have in you if you

- Blame others or things but never yourself.
- Think you have the best answer even though you don't have a lot of information.
- Feel victimized.
- Unbecomingly overcompensate as an adult for what you feel was denied you at puberty.
- Brag, boast, and claim credit.
- Second-guess people or presume a hidden agenda.
- Assume that you know it all and cease seeking knowledge. (One manager told me, "The problem with being so smart is that I think everyone else is stupid.")
- Don't listen because you think you're better, smarter, etc.
- Are narcissistic.
- Are rude, browbeat people, are self-centered, and abuse your power.
- Use "I, I, I," and "me, me, me" a lot.
- Drag your feet in decision making out of fear of being wrong.
- Think they need what you've got and that no one can replace you.
- Have a false humbleness.
- Are self-centered and must have it all be about you.

Everything I write about in this book—everything in life—takes a degree of self-confidence. Everyone wavers at times. At whatever level you are, let it be a personal goal to increase your confidence daily. Do not succumb to life, which tries to decrease it.

6

You Can Be Trusted

- Set your own ground rules and stick to them no matter what.
- Surround yourself with like-minded people.
- Repair a damaged reputation.

YOU DO THE SAME THINGS EVERYONE ELSE DOES IN LIFE: work and play. What sets you apart is *how* you do things.

You only get one reputation in life. Without a good one, the rest is insignificant in your leadership aspiration. Yes, you've heard of "seemingly" successful people with questionable repute who make it big. If you track them over an extended period of time, they don't last (sometimes because they are in prison).

Just as a bad rap lasts a long time, a good one does too. One newly appointed CEO was selected from a pool of talent by his predecessor because of the way he'd handled the funeral of an employee murdered overseas while on company business 23 years earlier. (Yes, over the years, he developed a solid track record too, but the "anecdotal" reason is the funeral.)

One CEO told me about a foreign assignment he'd had as a junior executive. Businesses in that country gave a departure pension perk that was disallowed in American companies. This young executive refused it when offered. Some of his peers didn't. Eighteen years later, this same person was one of the three in line for the CEO position. The other two had taken the money. The young executive who had refused it almost two decades before got the nod.

Your integrity is remembered a long time.

We have plenty of money to take care of any problems. We'll never have enough money to deal with bad press from low integrity.

Questionable character is the mark of death. Executive search consultants serving all industries will tell you that "companies hire for skills but fire for character." If you don't have unchallengeable ethics, nothing else you do matters.

There is no win, no advantage, and no victory that is worth even a blemish on your integrity. Nothing travels faster than a negative word about you. There's an expression that was around long before YouTube: "A lie gets halfway around the world before truth gets its boots on."

Fortune magazine wrote about GE CEO Jeffrey Immelt, who "stood before 200 corporate officers and said it would take four things to keep the company on top. Three of those were predictable—execution, growth, and great people—and the fourth—which was the one listed at the top of the list—virtue."

You have to have a handful of principles, and you stick with them. That's what leaders do.

What you do means little compared to how you do it.

It's like a religion or spiritual feeling.

If you are in a company, division, or group that has different ethics than you, you have four choices depending on your level of influence:

1. Get out.
2. Change the system.

3. Change the people.
4. Stay and suffer.

Burson-Marsteller polled 600 global executives and found that the CEO's reputation is worth at least half of the company's reputation.

I'd say that same percentage holds true for a leader of any group. As a leader in a position of power, you can have the temptation to step over the line of ethical or legal behavior. Depending on how much control and influence you have, no one is checking up on you. You can pull strings. You're at the top, and you see the loopholes. Being ambitious, you want to achieve more, make more. You feel the competition breathing down your neck, and sometimes you can be tempted not to follow your own rules. What you'll choose is your test of integrity.

A telemarketing company CEO sentenced to 18 years in federal prison for mail fraud, conspiracy, and money laundering said, "Any integrity that I had at that point in time went out the door. Gone. I had embraced the illusion that nobody could touch me. I believed I was invincible."

It is human nature to be seriously tempted by greed and opportunity, which sometimes leads to lying, stealing, and cheating. With 1 in 32 U.S. citizens in jail or on probation, according to Department of Justice statistics, there is a good possibility that human nature won out over a moral code of conduct.

That being said, the behavior needs to be pretty egregious to kill a career that spans over 30 to 40 years. Martha Stewart was in jail and came back. Bill Clinton was impeached and came back. Still, the reputation you took years to build can be knocked down in days and even minutes with such simple seemingly minor actions as tallying your golf score deliberately incorrectly, or putting an inaccurate number of miles down on your expense account.

If you've sidled off the path in the past, you can choose to be different going forward. Almost anything can be overcome.

CEOs like to play golf because the real character of a person comes out. It's only lore that decisions are made on the golf course, except for decisions of character. There's tons of golf etiquette that points to character. For example, you don't hold up the game if you're at 11 strokes and they finish at 4; pick up your ball. If you don't know the basic rules of golf courtesy and your own ability (e.g., handicap), but you act and talk like you do, you won't be trusted. ... If you record an inaccurate score for yourself, it will be remembered for the rest of your life. People figure that if he cheats at golf, he probably cheats on his wife and cheats in business.... If you act without integrity—in the office or on the golf course—you will be ill thought of, never asked again to participate, and talked about behind your back.

Junior Achievement and Deloitte & Touche reported on research showing that over 40 percent of U.S. high school students feel that it is okay, even necessary, to lie, cheat, or steal to get ahead. Since children learn what they live, what does this say about their parents—your peers?

Frankly, the world is not rife with high integrity, even in places where you'd expect it: business, politics, government, law enforcement, science, sports, research, religion, or charities. Regrettably, you can't name one area where there hasn't been scandal in recent years—or months. No wonder that students believe what they do. Sadly, me writing "have integrity" can come off as kind of quaint.

"I trust him" is what you want said about you. Anything less clear won't get you many followers or make you as much of a leader. The requirements to make this happen are (1) you deciding to never give a hint of impropriety in anything you do and (2) then sticking to your decision whether no one knows or not.

I'll commit as I say I'll do, and if I don't, I'll tell you the reason why.

Is a CEO who wants to beat the crap out of the competition, increase a percent of the market share, or withhold information that benefits a competitor one of integrity? You could say yes and no. Truth is complex.

The amount of crap that goes on in the world is immense. It's a fairly corrupt world. Business and life are messy. Integrity is relative.

What Does Integrity Mean?
What Does It Look Like?

If you choose to have it (because it *is* your choice), you

- Adhere to the Western civilization Judeo-Christian code of conduct with regulations and rules that have repercussions if broken.
- Behave consistent with your values (of course, with this view, thieves have integrity!).
- Do the right thing, not the thing that feels right.
- Are talked about as a good person.
- Do what you say you'll do, make agreements/commitments and keep them.
- Behave the same in public as in private when no one is looking.
- Do no intentional harm.
- Follow your rules/principles, especially when under pressure.
- Can be trusted to do the right thing no matter what.
- Are not motivated by a fear of being caught.
- Are scrupulously honest; there is never even a suspicion of scandal.
- Obey the law.

It's easy to read this list and say, "Oh yeah, that's me." A test is what your peers would say if sent an anonymous query. Or, if in a conversation that you aren't part of someone is accusatory toward you, and another speaks up and defends you. "I know Sandra, and she wouldn't do that." There, you have your answer as to what people think about you.

Remember the teaching of your parents—if your parents taught you well. (Otherwise, disregard.)

"When I got hired for my first job, my dad sat me down to tell me what my employer expects: 'They pay you a salary, and you work for them the whole time. If you get finished with your work early, find some additional work. Always be working because they are always paying you.'"

Set Your Own Ground Rules

Purposefully decide on and put down on paper your own rule(s), motto, or standard to live up to. If you do not know what you stand for, how will others? It can be as simple as, "I will not lie, cheat, or steal and will do what I say I'll do, no matter what." There, that's it. If you want to go a step farther, you could tattoo it on your shoulder blade in Sanskrit. But start with the commitment to yourself.

You can add nuances like

- I will not have backroom cowardice; that is, I will not be afraid to open up uncomfortable issues and instead cover them up.
- I will not straddle the line, waltz around, or put a spin on things.
- I will not give long-winded explanations or justifications.
- I will not intentionally mislead or misrepresent.
- I will not give a half-truth or fib or allow a strategic omission of information.

Stick to your self-selected rule(s) no matter what. Leaders create a history of keeping promises—promises to others as well as to themselves.

There is an old European proverb I like: "Tell the truth and run."

I left work at 10:30 p.m. last night. I noticed the trash can in the garage was overfilling, so I hauled it out and dumped it. That isn't in the CEO's job specs, but I saw something that needed to be done. After I use the sink in the bathroom, I clean it up. I don't have to do that, but I'm considering the next person who uses it. . . . At a new employee meeting last week I put my home phone number up on a flipchart and told them, "This is my home phone number. If this isn't the best place you've ever worked, call me and tell me so that I can do something about it." If I don't provide service to them, they won't provide service to each other or to our customers. That's how I view integrity.

You'll find it surprising what people think is unethical. If you're sick, you don't work, but you still get paid. A worker supposedly was vomiting from food poisoning, so he stayed home and took advantage of the policy. Turns out it wasn't food poisoning but alcohol poisoning. I wasn't going to pay him for an illness he brought on himself, causing others to make up for his absence.

I choose to be fair in my dealing. I realize what is fair in my thinking may not be fair in yours. You are obligated to bring it to my attention, and we'll talk about it.

Keeping commitments doesn't prohibit you from changing your mind and taking a different position if you learn additional information. You may revoke, but you don't renege. You don't flipflop because you're pressured, quarreling, under distress, or in an emergency or some other crisis.

Hold onto your pledge when you're having good fortune too—that's as much a test of character as when you're experiencing bad times.

Periodically, check yourself. When on the fence, ask yourself, "Would I be happy if what I'm doing was on the front page of the newspaper in the town where I grew up, where my high school flame, friends, and my mom and dad still live?" Or, as one CEO told me, he tries to make decisions and act "like my little brother is watching."

Surround Yourself with Like-Minded People

If people you're around get to the agreed-on end result but without integrity, the end result will lack integrity and so will you by association.

Put real energy into being in collaboration with individuals with integrity and high ethics. Surround yourself with people who have a sense of humor, who don't take themselves too seriously but do only take their work seriously. Be careful. When you're young, you can believe the banter of a person with bad interests that you can't find out about until later.

Concern yourself with your own actions in place of judging others. The fact is that people view the same issue differently based on country, industry, upbringing, culture, socialization, experience, and their own chosen code of conduct. Integrity, like beauty, can be in the eye of the beholder. State and stay with your position; do not concern yourself with judging theirs unless it affects your ability to stand by yours.

Take clear, deliberate corrective action if a person around you is a predator out to hurt others, do an illegal act, potentially cross legal boundaries, or hinder you from performing to your standard.

> *I felt like a business partner was stealing from the company when he took money to pay his wife commissions she hadn't earned. He thinks he's paying for effort expended. I have to worry about me and what I see as truth; I can't worry about what he sees as the truth. He doesn't feel he lacks integrity.*

You need to write about integrity with a small "i."

Human nature is highly susceptible to different interpretations. Accept that there are different standards and that misunderstandings will occur.

How to Repair a Damaged Reputation

Despite your effort to be the person you could play cards with over the phone, things will happen in life for which you are falsely accused. One man experiencing this said, "Trying to explain was like punching clouds" to no avail.

Sadly a disgruntled employee can write a letter and make up accusations of fraud. Auditors backed up by the Sarbannes-Oxley Act have been known to falsify reports. Despite falsifications or inaccuracies, you now have to deal with the issue in a series of steps while also following company policy and the law.

Get a personal meeting with the appropriate individual within your company or organization to clearly explain the matter. Invite the accuser to be in that meeting. Use this approach: "I understand there are accusations about.... Here's the situation from my point of view. I want to hear yours." Push to get exposure and closure right then and there. Don't let either party off easy because it's uncomfortable to discuss.

When you are cleared of wrong-doing, have your company or organization make a public statement proclaiming your innocence.

Make certain that your accuser publicly apologizes. A threat of legal action may help to achieve this.

Educate your team—from coworkers to family and friends. Equip them to be solidly on your side by describing what happened. Be brief and clear and use humor or irony to communicate what happened. Accept that people will look at and deal with you in a "trust but verify" frame of mind for a while.

Get public support. Call or visit people involved and tell them the situation. Explain it in a way that helps them to avoid a similar situation. Use humor and irony. "You won't believe what happened to me.... "Again, be clear and brief, and then stop. If you go on and on, it looks like you are protesting too much.

When you speak about the situation, look and act good-humored and good-natured. Maintain a relaxed tone of voice, expression, and demeanor.

Dive in. This is a good time to seek out a special assignment inside your company that offers the opportunity to prove yourself. If you were involved in community service or charity work before the accusations, step up your participation. Whatever you do, don't hide in embarrassment.

Maintain a professional, good-humored, and good-natured demeanor around your boss and the accuser going forward. If anyone gets a sense they've "gotten to you," scared you, or weakened your power, he or she may try again.

The final step in repairing a damaged reputation is to have patience. If you are right, attempts at damaging your reputation will go away. It may take years, but you have to remember: It's bigger to you than to anyone else. The same goes if you are wrong.

Without integrity, not much else matters. You will not develop trust, and people will not follow you. The good thing is that like attitude and confidence, it is 100 percent up to you regardless of your upbringing, education, and place of employment.

7

You Cause People to Follow You Even Though They Don't Have To

- Lead like others need, not like you need.
- Give credit to others.

TAKE ON THE ROLE OF LEADERSHIP *BEFORE* YOU HAVE the top level jobs and responsibility. Don't wait until that time because that will be too late. Work to positively influence others regardless of your rank or title.

Being a leader doesn't require an additional degree, losing weight, changing your hair color, or getting a toupee or a face lift. It does require specific, concrete, creative, set-yourself-apart-from-the-pack action in dealing with a diverse group of people.

Make the only change that matters, making changes in other people's lives.

You don't need power (from position or title); you need *influence* (from your personality and management style). With that, you can hire or recruit the best and brightest candidates, train, develop, manage, and motivate—all of which make up the number one downfall of CEOs today.

You basically inspire people to move mountains happily at their own will for you.

When I ask very successful CEOs about leadership, many respond with some version of "I don't know what that is." When pressed, they'll come up with something pretty standard, such as "being able to focus, set direction, and get a bunch of people to go in that direction."

Regardless of the table shape or size, there is always one person who sits at the head.

From my conversations with CEOs, I can dependably define *responsible leadership* as knowing what to do, doing what is needed at the time, and getting others to help because they trust you.

To be such a person, you have to be a stellar performing follower first. Then you must be lucky enough to have a leader of your own to learn from in the form of a boss, boss's boss, parent, mentor, coach, or business friend. You can learn from a good one, but you can learn from a bad one too—meaning what *not* to do. (Such lessons sometimes stick with you longer because they are more painful.) By osmosis, conversations, and experiences, you comprehend what's involved: You learn to understand and motivate other people.

After you do your time and you understand what it takes, you'll earn the right to make calls of your own, and you have to step forward with a leap of faith.

Karma kicks in, and your turn comes around.

If you don't have the confidence to do it, you'll be a lackey. If you haven't paid your dues as a follower but think you know everything, you'll be a B.S. artist.

People say that you have to be born with it. That's foolish. That's like saying to become a CEO, you have to be born with the ability. No, you learn it, like everything else. The ones who say they are born with it just got exposure earlier than the next person. That person was lucky to have a parent, teacher, friend, early boss, or neighbor who exemplified wise ringleader bearing and comportment.

What Does Being a Leader Look Like?

If you choose to lead (because it *is* your choice), you

- Think "we" instead of "me"; you put forth individual effort to create team-based wins.
- Have other awareness not just self-awareness and campaign for others, not yourself.
- Understand that being a leader is a service job—service to employees, social causes, and customers.
- Improve your people's reputation, not your own alone, and you keep it about others, not you.
- Grow others and share credit; you make it possible for others to use their abilities and take people to places they normally wouldn't go on their own.
- Don't just focus on your work but focus instead on the business as a whole; you get a large number of people moving in a similar direction where they're able to accomplish a great thing.
- Build a team of like-minded people around you and fill in gaps of what's missing in your own expertise.
- Take responsibility for your own weakness, even if only in private, and you get skills or put people around you with skills.
- Grow things and free up capital, and you see where the company can go and where you can be of help.
- Keep whatever team you lead moving.
- Do more than get everything done; you make a huge impact every day.
- Spark ambitions in others—both those under your direct control and those who aren't.

- Make choices, minute by minute, that make you better in your work.
- Treat your people as associates/colleagues, not subordinates.
- Have organized thinking, and you can take a problem or opportunity and sort it out logically.

Being the smartest, fastest, and best in some specialty does not make you a leader any more than being in front of a parade does. People choose who they will follow. The ones they pick treat them with respect, which translates into when something happens, their first thought isn't, "How does this affect me?" but "How will this affect my people?"

Although this book is about your own personal and professional development, true success in such development only occurs if you put that aside and understand, appreciate, support, and encourage the ambition of others.

Lead Like Others Need, Not Like You Need

Keep in mind that people are not like you are (for good or bad). You have to know your audience and know your constituents. It's shortsighted to think that since you are ambitious, insatiably curious, honest, hardworking, willing to take risks, and eager to produce results to move the organization forward that everyone else is too. They may be more interested in job security or spend more time on a hobby. Others (even with similar-sounding names, hairstyles, modes of dress, and job titles) can have dissimilar upbringing, socialization, education, work experiences, goals, motivation, and techniques.

Lead like others need, not just like you need. To find out, ask and observe to get to know what motivates them.

One CEO told me the story about a church choir leader in New Jersey with the same choir members for 14 years. The members are not paid anything; they have many obligations and have to extend lots of effort to be part of the choir. So why have they stayed with it for 14 years? The choir leader says, "I started out having the church choir be my own mission, but I soon realized that I had to help choir members fulfill their mission, not mine."

You can't just say to yourself, "I'm other-oriented. I care about my people. I understand them." You have to live it in small and big actions every day. The CEO of an international corporation had a gathering of employees and thanked them for their contributions in seven different languages. Small gestures such as this make a big impression.

Lead like you want to be led only if everybody is just like you. My style is "Give me clear goals and leave me alone. I'll call you if I need you." That's how I thought I should deal with others. But one of my people came to me and said, "You're too hands-off for me. I need more feedback," so I learned to adjust my style to others working for me. It's my role to be observant and ask people how they like to be dealt with.

I was recruited by the CEO, who was pushed out by the time I got on board. The new CEO never said, "I'm glad we recruited you" or even anything welcoming to me. He said that his leadership style was going to be one of repetitive organization rhythm, which I took to mean if you have enough meetings and documentation regularly that even idiots will start to fall in line. He had no interest in any approach other than his own. I believe you need diversity of thought, not just diversity of skin color, ... so I quit three weeks after I was hired.

In college ROTC, a test question was, "Should a commander be liked, disliked, or doesn't matter?" The answer was, "Doesn't matter." As beauty is in the eye of the beholder, so is leadership. All I want from someone to relate to me is with confidence. Neither of us has to be liked.

If you grasp the ambitions of others and help them to achieve and perform in a stellar fashion, they will gravitate to you—as someone worthwhile following.

If you make people around you more successful, you'll get pushed up by them because "a rising tide raises all ships." You'll get noticed and pulled up from above because the organization needs your skill to sustain itself.

People don't leave jobs; people leave bad bosses. You have the right to have a good boss or be the boss. Being a good boss yourself is more critical than having one.

A leader helps a group of people produce more than they could on their own.

If I used leadership more to advance in my career instead of just competence, I might have advanced faster.

You measure your leadership by the people who measure their leadership against yours.

To get my attention and be more successful, make yourself indispensable by how you get people to work with you. You being a star isn't sufficient; you have to make others a star too.

Give Credit to Others

When you or your team succeeds in anything, give credit to others. Glorify your people. Give more credit than they deserve for their contributions. (I remember being at lunch with a CEO where the meal was pretty dismal, and neither of us ate much of what was served. With a pleasant tone of voice, he thanked the waitress when she picked up the rather full plates of the inferior food instead of complaining about it. "I'm on a diet, and the food was so bad I didn't want to eat it, so the restaurant helped me out.")

Compliment your team. Brag about them. "I've got a great team. I want to tell you what Glenn did to help on.... I want you to know what Blake did on this.... " It doesn't cost you anything; it builds you up in your subordinates' eyes and with your superiors too.

It's common courtesy to share triumph; people don't follow anyone who hogs glory.

Nothing creative or important is ever attributed to being my idea.

If you think you get glorified for taking credit, you are an amateur.

I've worked all my life to get power to do things; now I spend all my time giving it to others. [I asked him how did he get the power.] How do you get it? You take it. Take it with some degree of certainty your boss would want you to or that you can convince your boss it's a good idea.

The general who sits on his horse and says "Charge" won't cause people to feel very good about charging.

Michael Jordan was a legendary basketball player because of his greatness but also because he made players around him better. The same is true at the office.

Three CEOs I've worked closely with were very similar in that they weren't flamboyant; they'd stand back and listen or observe; they had sort of a charm about them. They knew exactly what they wanted and how to make things happen. At the end of the day, they'd whipped your butt with work, yet they would pick you up, dust you off, and make you want to come back the next day and do it again.

You are not "made" a leader by your title or role. You "make" yourself into one when you constantly get good results through your ability to set an example for others to follow because they trust you.

8

You Accept the Need to Stand Out and Be Visible

- Do things people say can't be done.
- Get visible to a wider range of people.
- Stave off jealousy and loneliness.

YOU CAN'T FEAR BEING OUT FRONT. Just be sure to bring others out front too.

When you are visible, things happen. People seek you out because they've heard about you and your capabilities. They invite you into business meetings and conversations when they don't have to. Your name pops up when people talk and gets passed upward and outward. You are top of the mind and tip of the tongue. You receive calls from people you've never heard of inside and outside the company. You get endorsements from people because they know you. "Yeah, I know him. He's a good guy" is all it takes versus "Hmm, no, never heard of him." And you cause people to remark, "Let's get him before somebody else does."

It's very easy to become invisible. When that happens, headhunters don't call, bosses don't promote, and mentors don't respond.

Get noticed early in your career and preferably by the top people; that's how you get anointed.

Getting noticed does not mean unbuttoning the top two buttons on your blouse before you stand up to give your presentation. It will evoke a smile, but it won't get respect.

Being visible can be as simple as this story told to me by a client: "I remember joining this several-billion-dollar company years ago right out of college, and I happened to see the CEO unexpectedly walk by my cubicle one day. I stood up, went out to him, and introduced myself. He asked, 'Do you know who I am?' I said, 'Yes,' and explained that I had just joined the company, and he said, 'Well, keep up the good work.' And then he made a point to stop at my cubicle months later when he happened by again."

You can run with the pack and just go along, or you can leap out ahead. It's up to you.

Being visible does not mean that you embellish your work, are pretentious, show off, seek the limelight, have a popularity contest, or over self-promote.

Unless you fight against it, in business you can become like a rock in the river, tossed, turned, and ending up pretty much like every other one.

Being visible is not going to everyone at Starbucks and introducing yourself.

It's not who you know, but who knows about you.

What Does Being Visible Mean? What Does It Look Like?

If you choose to do this (because it *is* your choice), you

- Go out on a limb.
- Go the extra mile.
- Distinguish yourself.
- Resist invisibility.
- Care about what you're doing, not caring about being photographed doing it.
- Stand out but not grandstand.
- Share the limelight.

Take on the most challenging, high-risk, and meaningful assignments from the top leaders and the company. Do things people shy away from and say can't be done. Action and accountability make you visible.

If you're doing good things with no regard to accolades, you're doing them for the right reasons.

To excel, young executives need to distinguish themselves. Senior executives are the ones who need to be impressed, and senior executives are always looking for ways to identify talent. So do anything to make yourself noticeable by taking any assignment that comes. Many times a senior executive will need something done and be looking for someone to do a job. Unwise young executives look at this as being "dumped on" or the assignment as being "beneath" their new status. Wise young executives will say "Absolutely" to being asked to do what appears to be mundane. And then they will do a great job in filling the assignment, the senior executive will become more and more willing to ask them to fill assignments, and they will be more and more recognized. This is a first and important step in getting to

a position where someone is willing to trust you with their company or where you know enough to run your own company.

Do Things People Say Can't Be Done

If you get successes with a difficult customer, a new marketing initiative, a business development, an acquisition, a product introduction, or a joint venture, for example, you'll get known as the "go to" person whose name people volunteer when new opportunities come up.

Be willing to step up, speak up, and put forward what you did.

If you generate good results, let people know, not by saying, "I did this or that," but by saying "See what my team has done." Tell a simple story of accomplishment: the situation, obstacles overcome, and the outcome. With pride, name names and describe the efforts of others.

Don't brag about yourself, but boast about people on your team or someone else's team who helped yours.

I decided to be more candid and decisive than the next person—which can be risky.

Modest people often have a lot to be modest about.

The best way to be visible is to tell others how great your team is. You must toot everyone else's horn. And if you don't have a good team, lie that you do, and then go change your team. . . . The ones who tell me they are wonderful themselves always make me wonder if they are.

You better take credit if your [team's] work merits it because if it is the other way around, you will definitely get the blame.

I noticed one of our businesses was losing $250 million over the last four years. Problem was [that] the current CEO came from that business, so no one would speak up. I did.

To get noticed early on, speak your mind. If you follow blindly, you'll never get noticed. Articulate your view without being personally offensive. You're doing something right if you can get someone to think differently, especially if it's a superior.

Argue with your boss. Constructively fight for your project/company/ team; debate for the betterment of the organization. Be frank but in a respectful manner. Speak low-keyed. Don't be agitated, excitable, angry, or hostile or engage in a verbal gunfight. (That would create the equal and opposite effect: people avoiding anything to do with you.) The person who makes you mad controls you. That is not your objective here.

During the discussion, listen to what the boss advances. Present your point of view in such a manner that he or she listens to what you advance. Then you both advance to some sound thinking.

Stick to your convictions, but not so that you are perceived as being negative.

Don't be afraid of confrontation—but don't overdo it either. Never whine, but figuratively kick and scream, insist and demand. Don't be a sniper, or a politician while doing it. Hold strong beliefs and have the confidence to risk being wrong. It's worse to be a sycophant waiting to see which way the wind blows, reluctant to step up with a point of view. Be confrontational—be reasonable—with a smile.

Early in my career, I had a bad boss, and I told him, "You're not a natural jerk, but you're getting practice in it. No one likes you. You will be universally hated if you don't change. You lose your temper without cause, and you're a screamer." His jaw dropped. He sat there stunned, and then he said that he didn't know that, no one had ever

told him, and he asked to take me to dinner, and he bought me lobster. I'll never forget it. He was a big man, who came from a military background. No, I'll never forget it.

If my boss doesn't have a better idea, I'm taking mine. But I don't pick a fight unless I'm right.

Get Visible to a Wider Range of People

Associate with, consort with, and be acquainted with a wide variety of people. I hate the buzzword *networking* as much as you do, but the effort has merit to establish a relationship with, reestablish a relationship with, and reidentify with people you run into along the way.

The best schools, the best companies, the best network gets you around the best crowd and therefore the best opportunities. So it's worth the effort to go for the best.

In college, it's called socializing; in business, it's called networking. You do the same thing; it's just that your clothes aren't as sexy.

My wife encourages sleepovers for the kids and sports so that they learn to network from the start.

I know I'm asking you to leave your comfort zone—literally and figuratively. But if you don't, how will you discover who and what you'll be able to know and learn from? CEOs will give me a high five here: Your biggest regret in life will not be things you did, but the things you didn't do.

Decades from now, you may be different than you are today in a lot of significant ways. You may have a lot more money than you have today. You may have more money and more status and more power and more accomplishments. You also may have more responsibilities, more worries, more regrets, and more bruises. But underneath all of that, you will still be the same person who is here today, and it will be good for you to stay connected with the people who know the real you.

I'm the president of an industry association that meets with government ministers and department heads. Recently, one of my executive members referred to me as "our chief schmoozer." Humor aside, nobody sitting at the boardroom table tried to negate the sentiment. Had I really developed my networking behavior so much? Frankly, I like to think of it less as "schmoozing" and more as my focus to be seen as accessible, professional, and confident.

Anticipate discomfort. Forget that. Put your fears and apprehension aside or at least out of the way. Look at your list of possible things to do, and pick the scariest first; second scariest second, third scariest third, and so on down the list.

My dad told me as a young boy to always go into a room of people, pick out the most successful and smartest, and spend as much time with that person as possible to find out what worked for him.

This cultivation of contacts may not seem all that important in the crush of your daily to-do list, that is, until you need it. Then it's too late. If you put in effort now when you don't necessarily need it (or don't have the time for), it will be in place when you do need to call on others—then you'll be glad to have a network, err safety net.

When you are knee deep in your career, you wonder how you can take time away from your all-encompassing work and network. But you must make time for it. The 20 people you started your career with in 20 years will be in 20 different companies—and if you stay connected, you have an entrée into each of them.

One of my biggest regrets is the contacts I've let drop over time.

My rule is to follow-up four times. Nothing ever happens with just one contact.

Bruce Lundvall, president of EMI Music's Jazz Classic Division in the United States, signed Norah Jones. "People say, 'How did you sign her?' and I say, 'I returned a phone call.' You return every call," says Lundvall.

Jon Stewart, Conan O'Brien, Steven Colbert, and Denis Leary were all unknown struggling young comedians whose careers crisscrossed 20 years ago. Today, they are well-known comedians whose careers crisscross still. From day one, you start meeting people in your company, industry, and city—just don't lose touch.

Everyone thinks they know what networking is, but as soon as you start your career, you're building a network whether you know it or not—everything you do stays with you forever in some people's minds. I ran into some of my peers from when I started my career 20 years ago. They immediately started kidding me about how serious I was. It made me think had I been reckless with my reputation, that's what they would have remembered 20 years later too.

It's fun to stay in touch. Between 70 and 80 times a year I make contact with someone from my past—business or personal. E-mail is great. You're not interrupting anyone. You can say, "I was reading an article about . . . , and it reminded me of your work." Sometimes it turns into lunch or some business.

If people want to stay in contact with me, I try to accommodate. Everybody has a story; you never know what you'll learn. Unless I'm in the hospital, I'll respond. But the person should make it easy. Telling me I can only call them after business hours or on Saturday or Sunday is a mistake. Instead, say, "Have your assistant e-mail a time that's easy for you," so that I don't have to jump through hoops to be available.

Sometimes people become a "probligation"—meaning a friend requests help, and you can't say no. Today, it happens with people wanting to get linked in with you. Sort of social network climbing, where being connected with you gives them credibility.

Look for reasons to get in touch, stay in touch, and get back in touch. Follow up with whatever you started. Get out

- Of your cubicle
- Of your office
- From behind your desk
- From behind the wheel
- Of your comfort zone
- And meet new people or touch base with previously engaged people—keeping in mind that they are just as uncomfortable as you are.

People tell me that they like the idea of staying connected with people but find it difficult to come up with ways to do it. Here are some practical ways to build relationships that I recently used and the amount of time it took to execute each:

- I learned about a reporter writing a story about nonprofits in Chicago, so I called a CEO friend who heads a Chicago-based nonprofit and suggested that he contact the reporter to be a source for the article (3 minutes).
- I called the CEO of Krispy Kreme after I heard a new country and western song by Brad Paisley that referenced the product. I thought it would make my friend smile, and I suggested that it gives him a reason to contact Paisley and introduce himself, maybe get an autographed album for his teenage daughter in exchange for a Krispy Kreme T-shirt or ball cap (4 minutes).
- While shopping for some rock art for my garden, I found that a national artist at The Rock Garden was interested in placing a stone cross sculpture at a church. I offered to help and ended up getting it placed at the church my parents had attended when they were alive. The day it was being installed, I called the newspaper. The paper sent out a photographer, who put a picture of it on the front page of the local paper (couple of hours over a few weeks).
- When I was being interviewed by a *New York Times* reporter on my executive coaching practice, I volunteered the name of a CEO the reporter might want to interview for a different perspective. Then I called the CEO to give him a heads-up (1.5 minutes).

- I was given the opportunity to be on board a U.S. aircraft carrier, but a scheduling conflict wouldn't permit it. I asked if I could forward the opportunity on to some business leaders, was given permission, and five CEO friends went, and they, in their words, "got the experience of a lifetime" (2 hours making phone calls).
- I wrote a congratulatory note to the new mayor in town (3 minutes). He later contacted me for advice on a business situation.
- I introduced two single executive who are now dating (5 minutes with the guy, 15 minutes to convince the gal).
- I read a *Wall Street Journal* article about a friend who became CEO of a new hotel chain. I called to congratulate him and followed-up with a magazine article I'd seen about his competition (3 minutes).
- While staying in a hotel in Dallas, I called the manager and reported on a particularly good front desk employee. I thought she deserved recognition. She sent me a fruit basket when he told her that I had called (2 minutes).
- I e-mailed a reporter at the local paper and complimented him on an article (2 minutes). He later called me as a source for a piece.
- I phoned the editor of the local paper about a friend who started a new business, suggesting that it'd make a good story (4 minutes).
- I gave résumé and interview advice to a client's daughter after she graduated from college (30 minutes).
- I talked to a client's spouse about her ailing/dying mother (20 minutes). She sent me a poem that helped me during a similar time.
- I arranged for some vacant meeting space to be used by an outside organization's benefit event (20 minutes).

None of these actions required a title before my name or letters behind it. Just a little time, resourcefulness, and the ability to not focus on my interests and goals but rather on those of others. Every one of these examples I did in the convenience of my home or office. I didn't have to get on a plane, dress up fancy, or have a late night out. All I had to do was put a little thought and effort toward helping someone else get recognition for their work and effort.

How much is too much? If it substantially takes away from your work and family obligations or you're doing it for reasons of self-aggrandizement—it's too much.

Eighty percent of networking is just staying in touch. *Fast Company* wrote about the CEO of Ya-Ya, Keith Ferrazzi, as a "master networker. . . . He makes hundreds of phone calls a day. Most of them are simply quick hellos that he leaves on friends' voice mail. He sends e-mail constantly. He remembers birthdays and makes a special point of reaching people when they have one. When it comes to relationship maintenance, he is, in the words of more than one friend, 'the most relentless, energetic person I know.' "

When you take a break, say, for the bathroom, go (be sure to wash your hands), but then walk around and talk to people who you don't "have to" for a half hour. Giving each four minutes, you can engage seven people in a conversation in that amount of time—and learn seven new tidbits of information or help seven people with something they are working on.

Take a pause between meetings and phone home for four minutes. When you're energy lulls, instead of drinking a Red Bull, get up and get out of your work space. "It's very well received when the CEO schedules minutes a day walking around—which he does because I'm the one who finds the time," says one executive secretary.

If you initiate one contact a day, taking from five seconds to four minutes, you'll spend less time than it takes to pick out a tie to wear. You don't have to take more than minutes away from your obligations at the office or at home. Neither suffer. It's only minutes of resourceful other-oriented effort that I'm asking for. As Lu Stasko, CEO of The Stasko Agency, says, "You're only a phone call away from changing your life."

Stave Off Jealousy and Loneliness

If you associate with a wide variety of people, you stave off jealousy and loneliness. At the top, your usual mechanisms to connect with people are cut off. You're the leader; you're no longer a colleague. The people—your friends, peers, and mentors—who you hashed out problems with on the ascend are now part of the group reporting to you.

Some people resent that you're there and they aren't; others are intimidated by your new position. You're the boss, so you become the "collective enemy." Your confidantes change.

Some people say that it feels lonely because you've lost old friends; you have no one to talk to. And you don't have time to develop more friends, easily at least.

It's rare to be able to share sensitive personal company information that won't get shared through the building. When you become first-line supervisor, there may be 400 others in the company who you can draw from on workforce issues. That's how you learned—but that's cut off at the top.

You can't talk to a lot of people who understand your success. The peer/mentor in the company as you go higher up at the top of the pyramid is your competitor.

They thought I had someone to shine my right shoe and someone to shine my left. Not so. But I admit, for 15 years I never gassed my car. One morning I woke up and had to relearn where to put the gas in.

Because the dynamics of relationships change internally, you have all the more reason to cultivate relationships outside the organization in your own networking and mentoring relationships, where you can hash out problems without fear of exposure or negative consequences.

That's why CEOs join YPO, Renaissance, or TEC or become a part of peer groups and gatherings at Davos, Greenbrier, and Bohemian Woods. They have someone to argue with, drink too much with, and not get sued. They have an objective group like themselves who understands issues they're going through ... and have a really trust-ing relationship where they go to talk and get advice.

Leaders stand out. They have to be spotted by potential followers. When you are in the spotlight and you turn it onto others, you will be followed by the masses looking for someone to trust.

9

You Fit In

- Stand tall regardless of how tall you are.
- Slow down.
- Stop the droopy face.

As much as you need to stand out, you need to fit in. This does not mean that you change depending on who you're around. No, you have your predetermined (self-trained) style, you're flexible, but you're also consistent. Everyone gets the same person, or else you're a phony.

As much as this book is about differentiating yourself, it's also about fitting in—at least to a degree.

There is a picture we all carry around in our head of a person we deem memorable, impressive, credible, genuine, trusted, liked, confident, competent, comfortable, cool, calm, collected, and charismatic. Pause and try to recall someone who fits this description. It could be a boss, a public figure, a priest, or a character's role on television. Likely, in your mental portrayal, the person stands relatively straight, not hunched; is physically calm, not jittery; has an agreeable countenance and suitable dress; and makes you feel at ease.

You can be that person in this picture—err, you *have* to be if you want followers, because they share a similar idea.

Since you're being read, give them what you want them to read. Language is too slow in expressing complex thoughts or opinions, whereas a physical impression happens in a blink. Nonverbal messages speak to hearts, not heads. Words play a very small role in telling people about you.

In a matter of seconds, people either shut you out of or invite you into their circle.

People above, below, and alongside you watch, listen, and follow each move you make. Lots of minutiae are studied and discussed: the car you drive, the shoes you wear, your hairstyle (or lack thereof), and whether you put your recycling in the right bin in the company cafeteria.

There was a photo in the newspaper of me with Bill Gates and the governor. I noticed as I walked around office the next day that four or five people had tacked it on their wall. It's a smaller level of Hollywood. Instead of paparazzi, it's your employees following you.

Sitting in a review, someone reached over and pulled a dry cleaning tag off the belt loop of my pants that was hidden under my blazer. The person was studying me so completely, he spotted it. His comment to me, "Well, we know your pants are clean anyway."

You have to listen to what you say out loud. People take you very seriously. I used to be quick-witted and sort of flip, but now I have to preface comments so that people don't commit suicide.

If you elect to sit in the back of the room in an important meeting, don't talk to top management, and keep your head down so as not to be a target, you'll still get noticed, but for the wrong thing!

Theatrics are required in a leader. When things are not going well, you can (1) show it or (2) not show it. There is play pretend needed as an adult, just as you did as a child. When you were a kid, you acted out your dreams. You dressed and spoke like a cowboy, an actress, or a fireman. Similarly, as a leader, you need to act out being a leader.

Talk yourself into it. Remind yourself. Say, "I'm going into this, and here's how I have to behave."

A company video conference showed one manager who sloppily slouched throughout the meeting. A short time after the conference, he was demoted a pay grade and ultimately let go because people couldn't forget and get past the mental picture of him. He should have acted more interested

People believe what you show them, not tell them. You need to "look" like what people have come to expect in a leader. It's not in the clothes you wear (that's only a small part of it) or an accoutrement of power around you, but it's your bearing, manner, and comportment that cause people to have confidence in you and your decisions.

You're scared all the time, but you have to hide it. It's the price you pay to play the game.

It's a little like the tinsel-town description of acting: standing up naked and turning around very slowly.

CEOs are not thrilled every morning when they come to work. Sometimes they've had a fight with the wife or the kid didn't come home the night before, but they can't be grumpy. . . . The day I gave the best speech of my life, according to my staff, was the day after my life had started to fall apart, having been told I might have to file for bankruptcy. Regardless of how I felt, I couldn't show it.

When talking about 9/11, President Bush said, "I had to act as calm and resolute as possible because I knew people were watching." And this is not only reserved for modern-day presidents. President Washington was described by a biographer as a "master of political stagecraft. All his life,

Washington was mindful of his physical presentation, from the uniforms he designed and wore to the way he sat on a horse."

Acting isn't lacking genuineness. It's keeping rhetoric and actions consistent with the message you want to convey.

> *What I learned from Harvard was how to behave as though I had gone to Harvard.*

Theatrics live in all parts of life. Politicians, for example, are taught that when soliciting votes in restaurants on the campaign trail; (1) you approach the table, squat, and get to eye level; (2) make a joke about weather or food in general, not the restaurant's; (3) answer a question or two; and (4) ask for their vote, thank them, and move on.

In the book *Jimi Hendrix: Electric Gypsy*, there is a letter that Jimi Hendrix wrote to his father:

> *Dear Dad,*
>
> *I still have my guitar and amp, and as long as I have that, no fool can keep me from living. There's a few record companies I visited that I probably can record for. I think I'll start working toward that line because actually when you're playing behind other people, you're still not making a big name for yourself, as you would if you were working for yourself. But I went on the road with other people to get exposed to the public and see how business is taken care of. And mainly just to see what's what, and after I put a record out, there'll be a few people who know me already and who can help with the sale of the record.*
>
> *Nowadays people don't want you to sing good. They want you to sing sloppy and have a good beat to your songs. That's what angle I'm going to shoot for. That's where the money is. So just in case about three or four months from now you might hear a record by me which sounds terrible, don't feel ashamed. Just wait until the money rolls in because every day people are singing worse and worse on purpose and the public buys more and more records.*

I just wanted to let you know I'm still here, trying to make it. Although I don't eat every day, everything's going all right for me. It could be worse than this, but I'm going to keep hustling and scuffling until I get things to happening like they're supposed to for me.

Tell everyone I said hello. Leon, Grandma, Ben, Ernie, Frank, Mary, Barbara and so forth. Please write soon. It's pretty lonely out here by myself. Best luck and happiness in the future.

Love, your son, Jimmy

According to recent studies, 55 percent of communication is body language; 38 percent is tone, tempo, and volume. People study your demeanor, comportment, eye movements, breathing, gestures, lower lip, and voice. Ninety-three percent of what you're saying to them isn't coming out of your mouth (that's only 7 percent). Those same reports show that when there is a contradiction between verbal and nonverbal communication, the nonverbal is believed over the voiced.

Do not think that

- You are the exception to the rule.
- Competence alone will get you ahead.
- Competence will supersede "soft killers" such as bad breath, smoking, and procrastination.

You have to always be "on." At my company, there are lots of married couples but with different last names. People don't always realize the person they are talking to and what they are saying might have a negative fallout because of pillow talk that night.

He looks as though he's been a leader all his life.

A moment can turn into a memory that lasts forever—for good or bad.

What Does Intangible Fuzzy "Fitting In" Mean? What Does It Look Like?

If you choose to do this (because it *is* your choice), you

- Give people what you want them to read and ensure that the message you send is the one you intend.
- Convey a positive attitude—an intensity in carriage, stance, walk, and posture.
- Have exceptional executive presence.
- Act like a leader even when you don't feel like it or are tired, mad, or sad.
- Knock down barriers to effective communication by your demeanor.
- Get described as memorable, impressive, credible, genuine, trusted, liked, cool, calm, collected, charismatic, comfortable, competent, and confident.

There are numerous physical descriptors that we use in our language to suggest character, such as, "He can stand on his own two feet," "She looks you in the eye," "He is level-headed," and "She rises to the occasion," for example.

What we're trying to say when we use such language is that the person is self-reliant, honest, has common sense, and will step up (to use another physical description!) when necessary.

You can know in your heart that you are all those things, but if you can't stand solidly on your own two feet, look people in the eye, keep your head level, and literally rise to the occasion, no one will ever know!

How do you stand on your own two feet? Don't lean against a wall, a desk, or a lectern. Don't cross your arms over your chest or stuff your hands into your pockets. Stand with your weight equally balanced, knees flexed, and arms held loosely at your sides so that you are free to gesture while looking grounded and energetic. It may not feel comfortable, but it looks comfortable.

How do you look 'em in the eye? Don't divert your eyes. Focus eye contact anywhere on the face that helps to avoid feeling like you're boring in on them but at the same time appears that you're looking them in the eye. When you watch the other person's mouth while he or she is talking, you'll be listening and actually reading lips at the same time. When you pause to think of a response, look over the person's shoulder rather than letting you're eyes rove up and down and not maintain that level-headed look.

How do you act level-headed? Don't tilt your head to one side as if you were laying it on your mother's chest for comfort—or as if you've just lost the opening football game of the season. Keep your chin parallel with the floor and ears balanced over your shoulders. Instead of bobbing your head in the affirmation, give one slow, deep, purposeful nod.

How do you rise to the occasion? When seated (with good posture), ease your rear to the edge of the chair, and get positioned over your feet. From the knees and thigh area, not the back and shoulder, rise up. Don't hunch over with your chest almost touching your knees as if to bow.

These are just four examples; there are a lot more physical descriptions that suggest character, such as "His head's on backwards," "She's a lightweight," "He's a heavyweight," "She sticks out like a sore thumb," "He's under my thumb, all thumbs," and so forth. Think about what your physical demeanor, posture, and carriage say about you, and make sure that they are what you want them to be.

Stand Tall Regardless of How Tall You Are

Visually straight posture is the quickest way to look confident. People who exude confidence are, deservedly or not, viewed as competent, all of which encourages people to listen to them and decide if they will trust and follow them.

Good posture exudes self-confidence, positive energy, and makes you appear more fit and attractive.

Caroline Creager, president of Executive Physical Therapies, gives posture improvement advice:

- "While you steadily continue to breath, lift your rib cage up and away from your pelvis."
- "Roll back your shoulders, and relax them down (ears and shoulders and hips should be in a straight line with knees bent slightly)."
- "Pull your belly button in toward your spine to elongate your midsection and tighten your abdominal muscles—as you steadily continue to breathe."

Not that it's fair, but taller people earn more money and reach higher levels in organizations, according to a CNN report—on average, $789 per inch per year more. (*Fortune* reports that 58 percent of Fortune 500 CEOs are over six feet tall.) Regardless of your height, you need to be an erect executive to fit the image of a leader.

The stance also helps you to develop core physical strength as you breathe more fully through an open chest with aligned internal organs. Every day you take around 20,000 breaths (according to Mayo Clinic pulmonary clinical research). To do it healthily, breathe in through your nose while your abdomen expands, and then breathe out forcefully through your lips with a silent "Ha!"—done whether sitting or standing.

The alignment relieves chronic aches and pains, migraines, aching wrists, sore neck, and a stiff lower back. "Good posture fights the natural dehydration of the spinal column as you age and instead pumps a steady flow of oxygen to the disks," says Vijay Vad, M.D. "Hold your head up high—unbought, unbossed," said the late Congresswoman Shirley Chisholm. And even Oprah Winfrey says, "Boobs to the sky, ladies."

If you don't stand tall, you look like you have the weight of the world on your shoulders. That's a look that started in grade school when you rounded your shoulders hunched over a desk and carried backpacks, and then it continued in adult life with laptops, heavy purses, diaper bags, and today, "your burdens."

Slow Down

Even when you're busy, take time to have a calm presence. Just breathe in, breathe out, and then repeat.

An "urgent presence" makes you look nervous, unsure, and even unintelligent and often causes you to speak with unnecessary "uhs" and "ahs," stammer, and repeat yourself.

Fear moves fast. One man admitted to me that his rate of speech depended on the state of his bank account; the more financially desperate he was, the faster he talked.

A man in a hurry is not the image you want to portray. A man on a mission, okay, but not a man on the run.

Slow down; if you're worth it, people will wait. There is great motion in all stillness. As the Willie Nelson song says, "Still is still moving."

The more time you give yourself, the more status people will give you. This doesn't mean that you have an "overt lack of hustle," as Bronco Coach Mike Shanahan described a "nonplaying" player he suspended.

Do things on purpose, with and for a purpose. Take your time in a hurry. Slow down; you'll avoid the "freedom of Saturday night and regret of Sunday morning."

Let the flack pass. To be more effective, calm down; let it go. A world-class track and field winner explained his performance: "I just slowed down and relaxed and won." This happened because in running, as in business, you don't strain and tighten up to move ahead—you relax.

Even the gunfighter Wyatt Earp was reputed to say, "Take your time in a hurry."

Hal Pittman, chief of staff to General Abizaid, former head of U.S. central command in Iraq, said: "I learned to slow down my speech patterns when I was a young lieutenant. I had an admiral for a boss who was from North Carolina, and he spoke slowly, but with oh, so much wisdom. At first, I thought he spoke slowly and deliberately because of where he grew up—but I realized that speaking slowly allowed him an extra split second to formulate the thoughts and ideas, and that is why he seemed so smart. I've tried to adapt that speech pattern to a degree and have had success with it."

Stop the Droopy Face

Now I recognize that there are plenty of reasons not to smile. There is illness, maybe in your family, maybe you. You may have had parents, children, siblings, and friends who have died or are dying. There is poverty, disease, war, injustice, child abuse, and puppy abuse in the world. At the very least, you have stress, depression, and loneliness. Life is full of sadness. On the other hand, you made it to work today despite the hundreds of other drivers on the roads who were talking on the phone, texting, switching radio stations, watching a video, drinking coffee, putting on mascara, or eating a Big Mac.

A smile, a smirk, a sour puss, and a snarl all start with the letter *s*, but the similarity stops there. Simple facial movements change the outcome and attitude of the conversation. A nondroopy face simply has a hint of a smile—a millisecond of time with micromovement that encompasses your entire face and makes you appear relaxed, competent, comfortable, cool, calm, collected, charismatic, and confident.

> *I've found it relieves stress, is a natural painkiller, makes me look younger, seems to boost my immune system, and I've been told increases my attractiveness. Why wouldn't I smile?*

> *Assertiveness is aggressiveness with a smile.*

The kicker is to maintain a relaxed expression on your face when you don't feel like it—well, especially when you don't feel like it. Don't smile only on an occasion that demands it. (Don't even chew gum around others because it inhibits all facial expression.)

People put on a crusty expression to keep you away, to project disapproval. People do it knowingly, which is bad enough, but they also do it unknowingly, which is worse. If you give a scowl with awareness, you're judging. If you are not aware of your expression, you are not a leader. Your task: Frown less, and give one smile to a stranger per day.

> *My first CEO had humorous eyes, and a smile seemed to play around his lips. He was very effective.*

I'm not looking for a face-splitting "permagrin" or a "mouth open like a freshwater trout," nor the use of "happy faces" or other such codes or "emoticons" in your correspondence. Just do a "half-smilette," where the corner of your mouth turns upward. Do this, and then just breathe in and out several times to get the feel of it.

Get away from the dour, empty face.

The confidant facial expression is inviting, shows basic humanity, and hopefully reflects a life well lived. *Nondroopy* faces look cooperative, optimistic, relaxed, and like things are "sinking in" instead of "bouncing off." In addition, they produce positive feelings in the brain for both the giver and receiver.

Just think of your smile as an inverted scowl—if that makes it easier!

Individuals who lack confidence are stingy with smiles—as if they've already used up 12 of their 20 allotted ones for the day! (Or like Louis L'Amour wrote about a gunfighter, "A 20-foot stare in a 10-foot room.")

There's the story that's told about a much-sought-after Southeast Asian guru who people traveled long distances at great effort to join in meditation study. Once there, the advice he gave his followers was: "Sit and smile."

> *A mouth:*
> *Everyone has one, and they are all good and bad at different things.*
> *When you open it, you are telling the world who you are.*
> *When you keep it closed, you do the very same.*
> *It's the only body part that can speak for itself.*
> *—Rembrandt, oral health advertisement*

Think about a friendship or romance in your life. It likely started because the person smiled at you. The smallest facial expression can change your life. It can be lifesaving too. Next time you're a hospital patient, make it a point to smile through your pain. Although this is unscientific research, from first-hand experience, nurses will more quickly and receptively come into your room when you call if they know they'll be greeted with a pleasant demeanor.

Experts say that 2 percent of people are "face blind," like color blind, unable to distinguish expression. But 98 percent aren't, so it's a mistake to treat 98 percent of the population like they aren't seeing and reading your face. They are. Your parents created your face, but you create your expression. Like most everything in this book, it's *your* choice. Choose well.

Pay Some Attention to Your Wardrobe

It's more important how you wear apparel (i.e., posture and carriage) than what you wear. But why create an unnecessary obstacle for yourself with inappropriate, ill-fitting, or unkempt clothes?

As a leader, you represent the company, employees, and even the economic situation in the country—all by your dress. "You can't dress shabbily." (Yes, I too know of some Internet CEOs who take pride in meeting with billionaire investors in their T-shirts and cut-offs, but few can get away with that over the long haul.)

> *When I go to the mall, I guarantee someone will come up to me. It cracks my kids up. I used to dress like a slob, but now I consciously look better . . . and I have to shave every day too. . . . One of my people came up on Monday and said, "I saw you at Ace Hardware over the weekend. I've never seen you in jeans."*

> *Dress like you're interviewing every day—for a job a few levels up.*

Women would serve themselves better if they *stayed away* from tight shirts or skirts, low necklines (collared blouses are best), bra straps that show (even if fancy), superdangly earrings, lots of name labels, dresses that could pass as slips, mismatched purses and shoes, contrasting lipstick and nail polish, and loud colors.

Men would serve themselves better if they *stayed away* from the "human hamper look"—sloppy, untucked or wrinkled shirts (collared shirts are best), sagging socks, unshined or rubber shoes, accessories that overpower (better to stick with a belt, a wedding band, and a watch instead of additional bling), and mismatched belts and shoes.

Now, if you're a business legend, you can get away without the expected business uniform. One of my clients talked about running into a legendary Internet CEO in a local bakery recently getting a birthday cake for his daughter. "He was wearing the same turtleneck and blue jeans that he wore 20 years ago when I worked with him!"

Whatever clothes you choose to wear, they fit and hang on you better if you stay in reasonable shape. The highest-net-worth people maintain their ideal average body weight (according to height) over 40 years of age (the time in life most gain around five pounds per year) Studies show that dropping from 275 to 175 pounds adds $13,000 per year to your salary. (There are little tricks to hide the extra pounds. For example, if you button the top jacket button, you'll "lose" 20 pounds, according to men's clothing experts, or wear shirts cut fuller rather than tightly.)

I don't look like an aging Abercrombie & Fitch model, but I do try not to look like a dork in my workout clothes.

You can't be 20 pounds overweight and come into a job acting like you can be lean and mean in getting the job done. You don't represent vibrancy.

"I'd rather have someone wear a shabby tie and a five-year-old suit than have weak material and five-year-old concepts," said one CEO about the importance of clothes. I agree. The last thing I want people to say about you (as was said about one ambitious manager) is: "From the shoes he wears to the car he drives, it's all scripted, and it's too smooth." I just don't want something so insignificant to be a derailer: "He looks like a slob."

Beyond Shaking Hands, Reach Out and Touch

You can be in touch, stay in touch, get in touch, and sometimes get back in touch. But you do have to literally (and figuratively) touch *despite* how uncomfortable it makes you feel, the potential for misinterpretation, the risk of disease, the fact that others may not do it, what you've been taught, and what you've experienced in the past.

If a picture paints a thousand words, appropriate touch conveys 10 times that.

One day, out of nowhere, I reached out and touched him. He crystallized. He diminished into powder.

In Hollywood, people touch you not because they like you, but to see how soft you are before they eat you alive.

The contact I recommend is not a lascivious cop-a-feel, fondle, grope, power-play, or hit. It's calmly, purposefully reaching out and deliberately touching on an appropriate part of the body—generally from the wrist to the shoulder. (As you get more globally aware, you'll discover the variation of acceptability throughout the world.)

Both men and women should extend a hand to shake regardless of the other person's age, sex, race, rank, or culture. Clasp (your dry) palm to palm, not fingers to palm, with enough extended pressure to notice a connection being made. (Don't be so tentative that it feels like you're testing a mango for ripeness.)

If you decide to hug someone, to minimize it being misinterpreted (as anything can be), you can say, "I want to hug you in thanks for the excellent work you've done." Clasp their right hand, like a typical handshake, and then plant your left arm on the top of the person's spine. Lean in, but chests need not touch, nor pelvises. Turn your head considering the height differences so that you don't brush your face/lips against the person's face, collar, or ear—unless you're also going for a kiss. Hold the embrace a split second. Retreat while still clasping the right hand, step back, pause, and release the clasp.

If you don't want to hug but want to do more than a handshake, use your left hand to grasp the other person's wrist, elbow, or shoulder while shaking hands (the higher up you go, the more connection this represents).

A client recalled a boss he had early in his career. "He had varying levels of recognition that he'd give to people, starting with a positive comment, then a handshake, then a high five, and finally, a bear hug. I only got to the high five before I left for another job."

To receive someone else's touch, assume that it's well intended. Don't act as if you're being zapped by a stun gun, and don't pull back—in fact, lean into it, accept it, and reciprocate if you choose.

If you don't want to be hugged or kissed, extend your handshaking arm out farther and faster, step back, have a relaxed smile on your face, and gently extend a stiff arm (meaning keep it outstretched). Don't let the person come into your space. If he or she catches you off guard once, don't let it happen again. If he or she persists, tell him or her, with a pleasantly assertive manner, "I like to handshake, not hug or kiss." No explanation is required.

According to the Centers for Disease Control and Prevention (CDC), germs can live on hands and surfaces such as door knobs, railings, and computer keyboards for up to two hours. Estimates show that only one in three people wash their hands after using the bathroom. Maybe that's why the fist bump is in vogue.

Don't ruffle someone's hair, pat someone's cheeks (either pair), rub a pregnant woman's belly, touch yourself (i.e., any part of your body parts), or do unnecessary grooming gestures, such as when you nervously straighten your tie, adjust your cuffs, tug at your belt, pull up your bra strap, straighten your slip or pantyhose, or brush imaginary lint off your clothes.

Leaders stand out. How else will people know who to follow? Being visible means that you're being watched, so make sure that the message you send is the one you intend. But leaders also know to fit in—fit into the expected persona of a leader.

10

You Develop Others to Take Your Job

- Give acceptance but do not tolerate poor performance.
- Let people make mistakes.
- Develop successors.

EVERYONE DESERVES TO BE DEVELOPED. It's up to each individual to do it for himself or herself, but if you want to be a leader, you create an environment that intensely fosters it. Not all whom you help will "rise to the occasion" and fulfill their destiny, but some will.

Who gets developed? Talented people who are needed to meet strategic goals, those deserving a reward, those you want to retain, those who ask, and very important, those who can take your job so that you can get pushed up.

> *I was hard-charging, self-sufficient, and self-motivated. It took me a long time to realize that my success would be measured by getting others to succeed rather than just myself.*

I found out that your job performance is measured not by your productivity but by the productivity of others you influence. In other words, unit productivity is more important than individual productivity. I fired the best salesman in the company, and sales went up because his work was all about him and not the organization as a whole. I made the mistake personally as a kid. I didn't understand why I didn't get promoted because I was the star engineer. When I changed to another orientation, my promotion situation changed.

Like in hockey, the stats they keep are goals *but* assists *also. That is the single most important thing to get promoted.*

Developing others is the highest calling of leadership. Achievement is not just about you; it's about what you help others accomplish too.

You get pulled up from above when top management sees that you develop and invest in others, and you get pushed up from below by those you grow and develop. If you mistakenly think that it's all about you and your contribution, you will fail. You'll cause others to fail by your poor example. And you'll play a big part in the organization failing because you've hindered the development of people necessary to keep the machine running and producing.

What Does Invest in Others Mean? What Does It Look Like?

If you choose to develop others (and it *is* your choice), you

- Are supportive of everyone.
- Set a good example to emulate because as a leader people likely will do whatever you do.
- Make others feel as important as you or other people are; they'll work harder and give you more help.
- Let people make mistakes and have setbacks and disappointments to learn from.

- Don't micromanage.
- Make people unafraid to challenge your thinking.
- Are consistent.
- Say you're wrong when you are.
- Give big challenges to people so that they can learn and grow.
- Remember that people work for more than money or title; they want to be a contributor to something important, good, and worthwhile.
- Make note of others' accomplishments and successes; they can't always toot their own horn but sure like it when you do.
- Provide opportunity for career advancement.
- Never resort to "Don't forget for a moment that I am your boss and you'll do as I say as long as you're here, or you won't be here long."

Give Acceptance but Do Not Tolerate Poor Performance

To develop others, start by taking on an attitude of giving acceptance. As you have a right to expect acceptance from others and feeling broadly adequate, you have an obligation to give acceptance to others and maintain their self-esteem.

This means that you choose not to judge others' motives or character, only their behavior. You have no hidden agenda, work with a clean slate, have good "forget-ability," and tune out a lot. You recognize no divisiveness because of race, title, or history. Do not assume evil intentions on the part of others; understand that there are just differences. Be reasonable, decent, considerate, and respectful of others; control your judgment, rage, or anger. You understand the inherent equality of all humans.

Confident people give acceptance; insecure and paranoid people do not.

So how do you do it? Start with the attitudinal goal to do all you can to maintain the self-esteem of others. This is your number one job in life, much less in business. Every individual's desire in life is to feel good about himself or herself; you cannot make people do better by making them feel worse about themselves.

You give acceptance and maintain self-esteem when you

- Celebrate, appreciate, recognize, and praise at every opportunity— the more public, the better.
- Return calls within 24 hours, even if it's just a message on voice mail.
- Keep your word.
- Refuse to talk behind people's backs.
- Halt the spread of gossip.
- Write a complimentary note to the parent or spouse of a subordinate who's doing good work.
- Send flowers to the spouse of an employee when his work takes him away from an important event.
- Meet with departing employees, regardless of level, to thank them for their work while with the company and wish them well elsewhere.
- Sit down with each new hire, regardless of level, to welcome him or her to the team.

Let People Make Mistakes

You'll accomplish a whole lot more with people if you see less of their faults.

Be an amused spectator toward their irritating habits.

Maintaining peers', colleagues', subordinates', competitors', and bosses' self-esteem is more important than your own precious image, plans, rules, or success or you being right, on time, and efficient.

People will soon forget what you've accomplished in life but long remember how you made them feel about themselves. (A much different philosophy than that of chess champion Bobby Fischer, who said, "I like the moment when I break a man's ego.")

You and your job are important, but no more important than other jobs in the company. Don't think that you or your work is above anybody from cooks to custodians, to accountants, to executives. Value and trust all employees as vital in the organization. Those people need to be, first and foremost, treated well by the executives. They are the basis of what will make your company successful. They don't owe you anything. You owe them everything.

⊰∞⊱

We're all the same rank. I'm just the one sitting in the chair.

⊰∞⊱

Never ignore another person, no matter what that person's role is.

When you give acceptance, the recipient usually lives up to it. Even the trainer for the winner of the Kentucky Derby and Preakness said, "I told him [the horse] he had to step up his game, and he did." If it can work for a horse, it can work with Rashid, Mary, Margaret, Rock, or Juan, too.

Giving acceptance *does not* mean tolerating poor conduct. Nor does it mean that you let people slide. You owe it to people to help them grow and develop. Do not tolerate poor performers. Tolerating subpar work is not giving acceptance. Address and correct (err, attack, if necessary) conduct, performance, and behavior. Don't attack the person's character or motive.

If you accept others' motives, character, and abilities, then you can deal with behavior.... If I doubt the motives or character of an employee, I fire them. In a colleague, I transfer. In a boss, I quit.

Set straight the behavior of others in a pleasantly assertive manner. Do not be mean-spirited; you can be tactfully honest instead of brutally blunt.

Be firm in your convictions, tough, and resolute while still talking to others like you wouldn't mind being talked to.

Think about yourself. A boss who tells you "This report stinks. You're an idiot, and I doubt your honesty" will get less from you than the one who says "This report is below the quality I've come to expect from you. You need to redo it." The first assaults your motive and character. The second maintains your self-esteem while correcting your work.

You don't mind your own work criticized, but you sure as heck don't want your character attacked. Neither do members of your team. We're quick to judge our own actions based on our intent and quick to judge the actions of others based on the outcome.

Generally speaking, whether they deserve it or not, give people another chance every day, all day long. You've been given a few more breaks than you've likely deserved in life. Assume good faith from those you deal with, even those you disagree with, because, in reality, there are five sides in every situation: (1) my side, (2) your side, (3) the reality of my side, (4) the reality of your side, and (5) the reality.

So be empathetic—imagine the discomfort of others. Step outside yourself and see how what you're saying feels and sounds like to the other person. Set aside your own concerns, fears, and problems so that you can explore someone else's.

Deal with people regarding their conduct and performance not with your or their emotional or mental state but rather in a pleasantly assertive manner. If you don't, you will be acting as their parent, not the boss, cause people to take it personally, and might get sued.

> *Employees want to be related to by their boss in a way that's rewarding to them in every way. They get mad if the boss doesn't relate to them personally.... People have said to me, "You're insensitive." That's because I'm not willing to enter an emotional relationship on their terms. Why? It's a legal mine field out there. There can be no emotional interchange. I've been sued so many times, and never when I deserved it. I bond in great moderation.*

Learn to weed out losers in business and in life. Losers are people bound up in their own set of personal needs, needs that interfere with their ability to function at a high level.

Studies by both the *Harvard Business Review* and *Fast Company* magazine show that people consistently and overwhelmingly prefer to work with likable, less-skilled coworkers than with highly competent jerks. Researchers found that if employees are disliked, it's almost irrelevant whether they're good at what they do because other workers will avoid them.

> *Every night I think of three things where someone did something nice for me or to me during the day.... I think about how it affected me and my life, why, and how they did it.... I do it to make myself more aware of the way people do things.... Because of this, I sleep better at night. I'm more optimistic and more resilient toward daily stressors. I become a better manager, more effective leader, can better relate to peers, and have a richer personal life.*

When you are pleasantly assertive, coworkers will be more willing to be collaborative with you, and you'll more than likely get bigger pay raises and promotions, according to research at the Harvard Business School.

Kindness and courtesy are not weaknesses. Being kind far outweighs being interesting or even smart.

Pleasantly assertive means that you address problems in a cool, confident, and uncomplicated way. You accommodate people but don't compromise. You treat them nicely, not shabbily. And you refrain from eliciting antagonism. Pursue problems vigorously, but with respect; say what you think no matter how unpopular. Make time for people even if you don't have time. You are friendly but don't have to be friends.

Pleasantly assertive does not mean that you are nonconfrontational and let people slide. It doesn't mean that you try to be everybody's buddy. It does mean that you create a learning environment, not a ring of fear.

> *You must be direct, upfront, matter-of-fact, and frank,* but *with respect, even if it's someone who makes your life a living hell.*

❧

Tough but fair. I tried that once. Didn't care for it.

Use many resources and avenues of learning for your people. Give them "stretch projects," early assignments, training courses, and feedback to rid them of bad habits. Log progress, give feedback, and plan the next step. Set the example, and support and reward their efforts.

Return to Chapter 3 to remind yourself how you can constantly seek information and turn opportunities around for others to learn as well.

If you think, as a leader, that you are doing all the investing necessary in your people when you pay for training, coaching, assessments, and so on, you are shortsighted. All that is inconsequential to people compared with being made to feel good about what they bring to the table. Letting them make mistakes so as to learn and correcting their behavior without attacking their character is what develops people and will cause them to follow you.

I won't let a person feel like a failure, which doesn't mean they can't experience failure, but I won't let them dwell on it.

Develop Successors

You cannot move up and along unless you move others up and along too. Prepare people not just to do your job but to be a leader in general. This is what was said about one CEO's outside of work activity by a board member: "Todd's a very good tennis player, and he used to spend time teaching young people tennis. That doesn't do your own game any good, . . . but that's how you bring people along."

People are sometimes afraid that growing a strong successor will enable that person to take their job. The fact is that you need one or two people who could do your job for you to move up/on. If you don't have successors, you're not doing your job.

Like water pipes, you've got to have people moving through.

It is a huge mistake to have no other option and limited consideration of developing one. It's a management failure if successors aren't in place.

You can't move up if no one is there to fill your void; you are not a leader if you leave people in the lurch. If your promotion will leave a void, and you haven't gotten anyone prepared, you may not get the promotion for that reason alone.

You don't have to go to the extreme of one CEO, who said, "I hire smart people so I don't have to do the work."

Succession planning experts say that a well-managed company has six C-level candidates for every C-suite job in the organization. How many do you have in line right now?

Small caution: With an attitude of giving acceptance, you will get burned. You can choose to view it as spending your entire career being pleasantly surprised—or sadly disappointed—by people. You can fear it, or as with making mistakes, you can learn from the experience.

> *The worst part was living with the disappointment of putting faith, time, and money in people who don't perform or leave my company for a job across the street.*

In a conversation just before he died, author Norman Cousins coached me to "Develop the ability to trust people. Do not be overly disappointed in your trust, even when misapplied. You must not let disappointment from anyone deprive yourself of all the wonderful things out there."

> *This is a little speech I repeatedly give myself: I'm not bothered by those who attack me as long as they are open and impersonal in their stand. I'm always willing to forget differences and forgive detractors. I have no grudges and accept that I'll have enemies as well as friends, disappointments as well as achievements. I accept the unfairness of life with grace.*

To minimize them disappointing at the outset, tell people how important the business is that they are doing. Make clear the importance of their work in the business. Explain how together you'll help to make it all even better and more worthwhile. Praise them when their work deserves it; correct poor work similarly.

To help people prepare to take your job, set a good example. You need your people to have first-hand exposure in how a leader gets pulled up from above and pushed up from below.

Act with confidence, and do what you can to maintain the self-esteem of others to build their confidence. Live and work with integrity so that others emulate and see that "good guys do win."

Manage and lead with an optimistic perspective. Set goals for your job, for now and in the future.

Constantly communicate what you know, are learning, have questions about, doubts, and need to know more about. Set up a system to give and receive from up and down. Establish communication processes that work in your job, your culture, and your organization.

Dress, walk, and talk like a leader, again, to set the example. Know in deep detail the job you do; construct a profile. Be good at the job yourself.

Have a list of requirements for the job—competencies, values, experiences, and skills. Update the job specifications as the job changes over time; validate your list against human resources. Understand how your job fits in the entire organization. Teach your people to be generalists too.

See how the job can, will, or should change in the next three to five years. Have a vision for the future, and help your people to have a vision too.

Be clear as to where this job adds value to the company. Keep in mind the culture—actual and aspired to—and what it takes to succeed in it. Point out the downside of the job too.

Encourage your people to see themselves in the job, to strive for it. Show them how to be visible for this and other jobs. Foster healthy competition.

Use appropriate assessment tools. Assess internal candidates; write up your findings. Coach, mentor, and sponsor individuals. Use your global network to become aware of external candidates.

Keep up the feedback. Determine the next step for each individual to get him or her visible. Make your recommendations.

Give each candidate an opportunity to present to senior management. Push them to do things they thought they couldn't. Invite them into meetings they normally would not be invited to. Then implement your plan to ensure a smooth transition.

Change your recommendations when additional knowledge, exposure, and experience are apparent.

My predecessor totally gave me his sincere trust and let me go forward. If I had a problem, I knew it wasn't a career killer to get it fixed. He gave me the reins, and I took them. He made me his full partner.

≈◊≈

He put my hand on the spigot. I turned it on and off, though.

Don't just develop someone to follow in your footsteps, build on what you've done, or be in your own likeness. You want to help a person know (and you need to know yourself) what the company needs in your replacement. At different times there are different needs. After a period of revolutionary change, for example, some consolidation and organizational skills are required to move forward.

As a leader you always want to have developed two or three people who could step into your job. You are more likely to be promoted faster if the change leaves no void in the organization.

11

You Listen More Than You Talk

- Think, prioritize, and chose before you speak and then only sparingly.
- Ask lots of questions.
- Tell stories.
- Use humor and be human.
- Be consistent.

THE MOST POWERFUL AND LONG-LASTING COMMUNICATION is disseminated by the smallest detail. You can talk, but a lot more is expressed by what goes unspoken. Unfortunately, most of us "say" things we haven't even thought of.

The biggest problem with communication is the assumption that it has occurred like you think it has. Be able to constantly, effectively communicate up and down with people who answer to you and with those who don't. You'll build strong collaboration in your group, and that makes your group stand out among others. You'll have less divisiveness and strife.

In a two million dollar project, $800,000 of it is caused by poor communication.

⚜

You can never not communicate.

What Does Being a Good Communicator Mean? What Does It Look Like?

If you choose to do this (because it *is* your choice), you

- Are aware of what you're saying (and saying about yourself) when you are or are not talking.
- Make people from the top to the bottom feel a part of the dialogue.
- Exchange information by voice instead of writing and by telephone instead of by letter or e-mail, to one instead of many—whenever possible.
- Use lots of media equally, comfortably, and effectively so that you can influence a large number of people at the same time (still, you know that there is no substitute for personal contact).
- Are always accessible and ready to listen; you give an audience and absorb more than you speak.
- Never raise your voice when expressing disagreement or dissatisfaction; you speak your mind in the right frame of mind.
- Deal with aggressive people and in conflict situations without drama, anger, or argument.
- Cause others to be better communicators.

Listen Quick and Long

The best way to influence others is with your ears. If you listen in a way that causes people to feel heard, you'll hear things right the first time, maintain the self-esteem of others, build better relationships, see nuances to ask about, and be able to bring up something the other person said at a later time. "Remember how you told me to try...? I did, and it worked."

I've always followed Will Rogers' advice, "Never miss a good chance to shut up."

⚜

If you quit talking and listen, you'll know what you know and what the other person knows. You'll find out why some people are good and why some are better.

Shut out other people and distractions, and stop thinking about what anyone else is thinking or your response. (Take off your head phones, stop texting, turn off your cell phone, put away your PSP or BlackBerry.) Don't doodle; fidget with your hands, arms, or fingers; squirm; body-rock; or get up and move around (like you have adult ADD). Instead, lean forward, tilt your head a little, give some eye contact, and maybe throw in a brow furrow; don't glance around or act bored, disbelieving, or disagreeing. Just listen to the person who is talking, remember what he or she says, and say some of it back to that person later.

Resist the urge to interrupt/talk/respond or blurt out responses (especially if you're posturing or self-aggrandizing at the expense of others). It makes people anxious when they feel that you are going to interrupt. Wait patiently; take a deep breath (well, several of them). Listen, even if nothing is being said. Ask, "Tell me more. Can you explain that? What do you think about that?"

Don't quit listening if you don't like what you're hearing. Pay attention to complete information. Try to make sense of the data, even if you don't agree. Not every misguided opinion needs to be corrected by you. Pick your battles, as they say. You'll create calm for both of you, and the other person will more likely listen to you also.

If you're being reprimanded, listen quite often, and speak in very short words.

⚜

I've been told that when I don't listen to others, they feel intellectually inferior. That's not my intent, but that's the result.

⟞⟝

Sit and listen and be attentive.

⟞⟝

Shut up and listen instead of being anxious to talk. People tend to reveal themselves if you give them the opportunity.

⟞⟝

As you mature, you listen more. You don't have to put your opinion out quite so quickly.

⟞⟝

Stand up to be seen. Speak up to be heard. Sit down to be appreciated.

When communicating, steer clear of

- Jabbering, telling, stating, bossing, commanding, posturing, and making an appearance.
- Talking but saying nothing.
- Gossip (any behind-the-back conversation that hurts, shames, humiliates, or implies negative speculation about a person's motive and character).
- Commonly used expressions in business with sexual connotation open the door for that type of response and a degradation of the conversation and respect for you.

Playboy's Hugh Hefner says: "The best line is really not a line. The best line is listening. That is to say: The best way of getting a woman interested in you is to be interested in her." (Not that my readers would be interested in such advice, of course!)

Think, Prioritize, and Choose Your Words before You Speak, and Then, Speak Only Sparingly

To get people to listen to you, be worth hearing. The higher you go, the more of what you say is analyzed, dissected, discussed, and scrutinized. Coworkers literally count the number of positive versus negative words you use or the number of times you use "I" versus "we." (Remember, what you say here doesn't stay here—this isn't Las Vegas; it's "YouTubeville.")

> *Don't talk a lot; that's the worst thing you can do.*

⟡

> *I get around 600 e-mails a day. I divide them into four categories, and I deal with them immediately, by and large. First are e-mails that I forward to someone else. Next are where somebody is giving me information that I need to cascade to somebody else with instructions. Third are the ones that I can read later on an airplane. Fourth are those that require me to respond immediately.*

Over 100 million conversations are going on at any one time on cell phones alone. It would be a good idea to say what you're going to say to yourself before saying it out loud. Consider how your words will be received; and then say the rationed, thought-out words to ensure that the message you intend is the one you send.

It only takes seconds to preview your thoughts and readjust your words before verbalizing them to someone else. To hear how you sound, dial into your own voice mail, speak like you would on someone else's voice mail, and then play it back. You'll end up not saying things you regret—or not saying things in a manner you regret.

Slow down so that you are heard and understood. One CEO told me that he was giving feedback to one of his people, and he said that something was "pithy." The person took great offense, hearing it as "prissy."

Control your speaking voice. The smallest difference in inflection, volume, or speed of talking causes people to think you are excited, fatigued, mad, abrasive, or arrogant. One study found that women typically talk in a higher pitch with varying tones to boyfriends to express affection but then use mannish vocal adjustments to sound powerful in business. Some people recommend that you speak very quietly, almost at a whisper, to force people to draw in to you to be heard. (I recommend neither.)

To avoid sounding husky, harsh, honeyed, thunderous, mousy, or shrill, use a pleasantly assertive, matter-of-fact, pass-the-salt tone at all times. Say whatever you want to say without saying more than you want.

Use Short, Sharp Sentences

Go for the crispest, simplest, least elegant language possible in instruction, reaction, and direction. Precise language is more convincing than hyperbole and more meaningful than clichés.

My son tells me he communicates through his tattoos. I tell him that won't work in the long run.

Use a one-syllable word instead of two or three syllables; use one word instead of four or five. Write and talk with direct and clear-cut conversation; insist on getting to the heart of the problem. Be fresh, forthright, precise, concise, and when possible, funny. Even with a forceful manner, you can still project warmth, depth, and a cool strength.

If the other person doesn't understand you, it's your fault.

Don't just dispense data; make a connection with people through material information, facts, and figures. Make complicated information simple to understand for a diverse group (e.g., age, culture, experience, education, etc.). An example of such a need can be seen in the creation of the Transportation Security Administration (TSA), which went from zero to 60,000 employees in four months, people drawn largely from the military, law, dot-com companies, and Enron. Management strived for the simplest, most direct, and understandable-by-all wording in every document they produced.

Without being tedious, tell people what you're going to tell them. Tell them, tell them what you told them, and ask them if they got it—in no more than three to five sentences. Then wait for a response; give people a moment of silence in their heads.

Speak plain English. Don't use buzzwords from your MBA school. You'll only impress other MBA schoolers. Ninety percent have no idea what you're talking about.

≈⊚≈

As a leader, before you embark on a conversation, ask yourself these questions: Why am I doing this? What is it that I want or need to say that is of value to someone whose time is as precious as mine? What is compelling about my message? How do I deliver my words in a way so that others can understand them?

≈⊚≈

You don't want to finish and have your people ask, "What did he say?"

Ask Lots of Questions Without Grilling, Interrogating, Challenging, or Playing "Gotcha"

Questions more than statements stimulate the possibility of effective communication. You cause people to be better communicators around you by asking questions of them, listening, and not interrupting. You find out what they want, but just as important, you reach out and make the uncomfortable comfortable. You get people who don't normally open up to open up. And you set an example for others to do the same.

Uncertainty is the only thing you can be certain of, and to make things less uncertain, you have to ask about them.

Make it a practice goal to ask everyone you encounter during the course of a day at least one question, and always make the first verbal communication an inquiry rather than a statement. ("How's your day?" is a little unimaginative but still better than "Let me tell you about my day.")

Who, what, when, where, why, and how will serve you just about anytime. But volunteer information about what you're asking so that you hold up your end of the social contract of "give and take."

Asking questions lets you test, test, test your way through a situation to avoid a gigantic setback. Barbara Walters says that when she wants to question someone in a pointed fashion, instead of asking, "Are you crazy?" she'll ask, "You know there are people who want to ask 'Are you crazy?'"

You generate credibility, trust, and likeability. You build relationships when people feel valued by you, so you resolve conflict before it escalates.

People will allow you to lead if you make it worthwhile and enjoyable to follow.

A client told me the story of her husband "John" and his first interview with a major financial institution:

> He was with 50 other potential recruits wined and dined by the brass to encourage the recruits to want to work for the company. John was amazed and awed by the larger-than-life shrimp at the buffet, as well as the rest of the extraordinary spread. The main event began with the 50 recruits seated around an enormous table with 15 to 20 company execs. They sat through a video and a few speeches about what a great place this was.
>
> Then the spotlight moved to the tremendous boardroom table, and the main presenter asked the recruits, "Who has questions?" The fear and tension among the young men and women could have been cut with a knife, and their minds raced with anxiety-laced thoughts. "What if I ask a dumb question? But doesn't it look bad if I ask no question at all?" and so on. One woman was randomly picked out of the crowd and asked if she had any questions. Her heartbeat sped up by many paces as the others breathed a sigh of relief. She looked like a deer in headlights and finally came up with a weak, "I have no questions." In response, the presenter asked, "How about the person to your right? Do you, sir, have any questions?"

> *The "sir" was John, whose mind was scattered. He was thinking that he was certainly not going to make the obvious blunder that the woman had made, but at the same time, he was drawing a blank. He opened his mouth and said the first thing that came out to him: "Where did you guys find such tremendous shrimp?" The room exploded with laughter, and the massive tension that had been hovering was released. Once the laughter subsided, John had cleared his own mind enough to think intelligently again, and he did in fact come up with an impressive question. John was one of eight people who received a job offer after the recruiting event.*
>
> *About a year later, he had a meeting with an executive who said, "You look familiar." They couldn't figure out how they knew each other, and finally, the light bulb went off. The exec said, "I know, you're the shrimp guy!" John's gutsy and humorous approach made a long-lasting impression.*

Make it so that people are unafraid to question or challenge you. When questioned, answer slowly. Respond with an informed, incisive, candid, objective, and clear response. You also can reply with a question—not to irritate, be cute, or be cagey—but to clarify what the person was asking. Even an "I'm glad you asked that question" buys you some time to think about your response while flattering the asker of the question. (Everyone needs to have their self-esteem maintained.)

Don't be a "ball-fetcher" only meaning someone who runs off to get an answer when posed a question. It looks too eager to please and lacking in confidence.

A "Tell me about yourself" question, for example, in a job interview should not be answered with where you were born, what you're parents did for a living, what you did in school, who your favorite teacher was, where you went to college, what you studied, what your extracurricular activities were, where you've worked since getting out of college, what you did, what you liked, what you didn't, what you do for fun, and what your horoscope is.

Now, you may eventually tell them all that, but it would be better to answer "Tell me about yourself" with a question such as, "Would you like to know about my work experience, educational background, or my life outside of work?" In other words, make clear what they are asking. It sets you apart from others who don't and gives you time to think about answering the question they are *really* asking instead of what you assume they are asking.

When I start to sweat and my body gets really warm because of a tone of interrogation, I block out the emotional feeling and concentrate on listening to the words to try to focus and understand the real concern.

When challenged, don't jump on the person with all fours; instead, ask yourself, "Is it necessary to respond?" and "Can I improve on the silence?" Instead of "verbal vomit," where you spew out any nasty thing on your mind, take a deep breath (well lots of them, if necessary), bite your tongue (not literally, but it doesn't hurt that bad if you do), and keep quiet a moment longer. Look the person in the eye, and ask, "Tell me more."

Slow down when you're mad, put on the spot, feel defensive or trapped, or have hurt feelings. You might end up where you divulge, disclose, let down your guard, emotionally flash, confess, or "level" without a lot of thought with things that "crop up in your head."

Do speak up audibly, though. According to the American Academy of Audiology, more than half the population has some hearing loss.

Tell Stories

Instead of PowerPoint, statistics, facts, lists, intellectual rhetoric, quotes from authorities, boring memos and e-mails, or clichéd corporate communication missives, make your point, persuade, influence, engage listeners, communicate, arouse listeners' emotions, charge their energy, and inspire—through anecdotes.

To be a raconteur, keep coming up with new ones (don't tell the same ones over and over again because they lose their impact), use the right ones for the situation, keep them brief, make sure that you're going somewhere with your stories, and don't manipulate facts or exaggerate to make your point.

Understanding is a combination of facts and beliefs. People are complex; they don't deal with facts alone. Facts are shaped by the filter of feelings. Stories bring facts and figures to life, create an emotional bond, and bridge the head and the heart.

The best stories tell of overcoming adversity or a struggle. A sad story teaches more than a happy one because people learn more from mistakes than from successes. The best stories cause people to think, "Boy, I'm glad that didn't happen to me. That's so interesting. That's so right. I understand. I agree."

I was at death's door, and the devil said, "You remind me too much of myself. Get out of here." Some nurses were sitting up with me late one night, and I could hear some spirited conversation. I asked, "What's going on?" One said, "They have a pool going to see if you're going to make it." That's all I needed to hear. I got up off that bed and started walking immediately."

To tell stories, set the scene in a few words; then tell the struggle/obstacle/hurdle/setback and how you overcame it. Over 2,000 years ago, Aristotle wrote in *Poetics* that stories should have a beginning, a middle, and an end; complex characters as well as a plot that incorporates a reversal of fortune and a lesson learned; and be engaging by involving the five senses to draw people in.

Interesting side note:

Every Bond story has (1) intro of Bond and the villain, (2) villain and Bond compete in some sport/event, (3) villain cheats to win, (4) Bond cheats the villain to win, (5) villain captures Bond, (6) villain tortures Bond, (7) Bond escapes villain, (8) Bond seeks revenge on villain, (9) villain expires, and (10) Bond gets the girl. Or, as in almost every movie, introduce characters, get them up a tree, and get them back down.

Your stories improve the more you take out rather than put in. Knock out every word that doesn't count. To give you an idea of the necessity for removing unnecessary verbiage, consider that to produce a daily script for the *Colbert Report*, 80 writers boil all their contributions down to a 30-minute script. That same kind of cutting of superfluous information is required in your "script."

Understand that a story simply explains how and why life changes. It begins with a situation in which life is relatively in balance: You come to work day after day, week after week, and everything's fine. You expect it will go on that way. But then there's an event—in screenwriting we call it the "inciting incident"—that throws life out of balance. You get a new job, or the boss dies of a heart attack, or a big customer threatens to leave. The story goes on to describe how, in an effort to restore balance, the protagonist's subjective expectations crash into an uncooperative objective reality. A good storyteller describes what it's like to deal with these opposing forces, calling on the protagonist to dig deeper, work with scarce resources, make difficult decisions, take action despite risks, and ultimately discover the truth. All great storytellers since the dawn of time—from the ancient Greeks through Shakespeare and up to the present day— have dealt with this fundamental conflict between subjective expectation and cruel reality.

—Robert McKee, award-winning writer, director, and screenwriting lecturer for Harvard Business Review

---

Use Humor

Humor is the bedrock of humanity (that and thoughtfulness). It's universal communication. Learning to use judicious humor is a serious part of your business leadership development. When there is tension, the only good emotion to use is humor. Fear, anger, revenge, and retaliation aren't good. Besides, without fun, it's killing to do the capacity of work needed to be done.

Don't expect everything you attempt to come across amusing. People view different things as funny based on their age, life experience, confidence, and wiring in their brains. (Their not "getting it" is usually more about them than about you.) Even Hallmark Card's Shoebox Division (the humor division) tosses out four of every five funny verses presented to its editors. Professional joke writers for the Lenos, Lettermans, Colberts, and Stewarts of the world have, on average, 1 in 16 jokes that make it on the air.

Don't try to be funny; just tell a narrative with an unexpected twist. "Enlarge the trivial, and trivialize the large". Self-deprecate, self-mock, and self-parody.

You'll have a better career if you can make people laugh.

You should laugh heartily at least once a day—not at others, at yourself. Don't worry if they laugh too hard or hardly at all.

Humor is being human. You are a human being before you are a leader. Your career will go nowhere if you can't maintain the human factor. Communicate as frequently and as personally as you can; be as human and down to earth as possible.

"We all breathe the same air. We all cherish our children's future. We are all mortal," said President John F. Kennedy.

I want to assure you that I feel the same pain and the same stress and the same jet lag as anybody else.

❧

At company Christmas parties I act drunker than I am to be human and approachable. Now it's not all acting. Same approach when I give an extemporaneous speech: I get up there, loosen my tie, and speak extemporaneously. Fact is, I memorized the important parts, including planning some jokes to slip in.

When you use humor and be human, you change the energy in the situation, diffuse emotion, relieve tension, reduce burnout, improve morale, enhance cooperation, and even lower blood pressure—yours and theirs. You connect sooner and better with other people, especially if you're in a powerful, intimidating role (we don't want our leaders to be the funniest people in the room; we just want to see them as human beings). You minimize hubris and improve your health, from cardiovascular, to memory, to weight loss (medical experts say that every time you laugh, you add some time to your life).

Be Consistent

Present the same face day in and day out to all coworkers in a constant manner. Avoid the description given about one CEO wannabe: "He was riddled with inconsistency. He seemed dishonest." You cannot be one way one day with one persona and a different way the next.

If you are inconsistent, you create tremendous ambiguity, confuse people, and cause them to be inconsistent back to you.

Public Speaking Communication

Leaders speak to groups to reach and influence larger numbers of people. One CEO told me, "I made 70 speeches in 90 days." Whether it's 70 or 2 in the next 90 days for you, there is an ideal situation to positively increase your visibility.

When you're preparing your speech, ask questions about your audience. What's the makeup? Who have they heard previously? What is their state of mind? What would benefit them?

Don't rely on professional speech writers. Or if you do, tell them what *you* want to say. Before you accept a speech from a speech writer, ask the writer if this speech says what you want it to say. At the same time, write the speech yourself, and then marry the two at the end.

Then, as in all good communication, tell your audience what you're going to tell them, tell them, and then tell them what you told them.

Practice the speech out loud so that you can hear how it sounds to your ear. Practice by presenting to a group of fifth graders, if possible, or at least to your 12-year-old niece. If you can reach them on a visceral, personal, and emotional level, you'll be able to deal with any executives.

You needn't do what I saw in one politician's notes, "Choke up on page three, and brush away a tear on page four."

When you're delivering your speech, your first remark should be an attention-getting statement, preferably one your audience would agree with, to enlist them from the start. Then proceed with their interest peaked. If they trust you from the beginning, you can go on and say what you need to say in a fun, spirited conversation with the audience. "We are so fortunate to live the way we do and be able to gather together to talk like we are. I'm grateful and proud to get to speak to you about. . . ."

Use humor that is topical, tasteful, and pertinent to help establish rapport. The more you generate some laughs or at least snickers, the smarter they will think you are, and the more you'll relax and do better.

To avoid being "scared scriptless," provide a series of points or propositions in numbered or logical sequences. Go for three points, three things to take away, three top tasks—three is magic for being remembered and repeated.

Incorporate stories of survival early on, where you, the company, or a group was pitted against another and won. Get excruciatingly personal, where you share honest vulnerability or private pain. Be honest; don't B.S.

Use rhyme, alliteration, even poetry—serious messages don't need to be boring. Construct sentences, phrases, and paragraphs to simplify, clarify, and emphasize. Avoid verbosity and pomposity. Use short, sharp, unpretentious wording to aid in the audience's comprehension and comfort. With major points, be positive, specific, and definite; avoid such words as *suggest, perhaps, possible alternatives for consideration,* etc. Write sentences that are lean and crisp and crowded with facts but not generalities and sentimentalities. Use no slang, legalistic terms, clichés, contradictions, elaborate metaphors, or ornate figures of speech.

Rule: ABWADUA—"Avoid buzzwords and don't use acronyms."

You create your legacy with different messages that stand out from the competition, especially with ideas others aren't talking about.

Just before you walk on stage, take deep breaths as if your chest were a swinging screen door.

The optimal distance between your mouth and most microphones is 1 inch, but the sound technician will adjust. A panel presentation may not have the individual microphone setup, so it's particularly important to position yourself accordingly.

When you're on stage or simply in front of people, don't move about a lot. Reposition only when movement is in harmony with the verbal message, and then, slow it down.

People hear based on your words and physical presence more so than just the words you say.

Make eye contact with individuals one at a time instead of scanning the crowd. The one-on-one eye contact makes you feel less intimidated.

Remember that today you aren't speaking to the room but to the world, so watch what you say on and off the stage. (It could be on the Internet before your closing comment.)

Use less time than allotted to you. You can always fill in the time with Q&A. (Don't cross your arms just before you ask for questions unless you don't want to get any.) Do restate the question so that everyone hears it, but don't answer to the person who asked it: Answer to someone else so that you don't invite a one-on-one conversation feel.

End long before the audience has had its fill.

Whether communicating one on one, to a group, on the phone, or in the hallway, make it about what you hear instead of what you say.

12

You Are Decisive

> - Make decisions yourself.
> - Sell your decision.
> - Review what happened.

BEING THE MAIN DECISION MAKER IS SCARY. Frankly, it's easier when decisions are made for you; then you don't have to put out the mental and physical effort. In addition, there is someone else to blame if it goes wrong. But the humungous downside is that you live under someone else's rule, and usually that someone else has less to offer than you do.

Every day, all day, decisions are being made for, around, alongside, and behind you. The more *you* can make, the better you control your own career.

If you are trying to be a world-class leader with integrity, optimism, and a desire to improve, providing results and developing others, you are in as good of a position as almost anyone to make decisions.

It takes confidence to put a stake in the ground, but that is how you get known. Even when you're wrong, you show the world what you're about by how you handle the setback, fix it, learn from it, and not repeat it.

If you want to stay in a pool of high potentials, decide to decide, sooner rather than later, and then rigorously debrief yourself about the outcome.

Decisions are a bigger deal than the work of inspiring, vision, selling, or leadership.

⮞⮜

Few decisions in business are life and death.

⮞⮜

Sometimes you have to close your eyes and say, "Okay, let's go."

Nothing happens without a decision being made. Others will make them for you, or you can be the one making them. You make the change you want. If you make the decisions, you just might get the results you want. The only differentiation between you and others is who will step up. If you freeze, you lose. Period.

Life is about making decisions. The question is how can two people look at the same data and one get it right and the other not even get it close? From judgment—making lots of decisions and learning from the experience.

The assistant to one of the CEOs I interviewed said of the executives who go in and out of her boss's office: "Good ones are very decisive. They know exactly what they'll do and do it charmingly. They are never wishy-washy. If wrong, they are the first to say maybe I didn't make the right decision, and they never point fingers. I can smell a good executive and a bad one right off. The bad ones are not able to make a decision. You need experience for making the right decision. Younger, immature usually don't have a clue."

In any group of people, there are only a few who feel broadly adequate to make decisions. Be one of those whether you have the responsibility or not.

If you're timid and fear "making a bone-headed move," you decrease others' confidence in you. If you hold back, you let others make decisions that you have to live with.

Pull the trigger: yes or no. You can't half pull, can't half lead.

What Does Being Decisive Mean? What Does It Look Like?

It's up to you to seek it out, and when you do (because it *is* your choice), you

- Think; then act.
- Take the lead; take the charge.
- Make up your mind.
- Focus and set a goal/objective.
- Are quick on your feet versus sluggish to move.
- Get others on board.
- Develop judgment.

Decide to Decide; Then Do It

Look at where you are and where you want to go. A well-defined problem that is communicated in a ruthlessly simple manner is a problem half-solved. Think about how to get there, start to go toward it, and periodically check your progress.

Think independently, but ask questions of others. Get and review the cold, hard facts. Gather as much information as possible talking to constituents, contacts, and mentors; do research and read. (If you have a broad network of contacts, a pool of mentors, and a diverse team around you, you'll get different input from which to make your choice.)

Consider the pros and cons, plusses and minuses, strengths and weaknesses, and opportunities and threats. Look at the situation from the perspective of all constituents involved, both inside and outside the company—customers, vendors, management, plant, administrative, human resources, financiers, distributors, competitors, etc.—and determine how it will affect them. Brainstorm with people connected and talk to people not connected or related to the situation (bartenders and hairdressers are used traditionally). Think of an analogy that is similar to your situation (e.g., a hospital marketing guru studied how airlines fill seats to come up with a new idea about how to fill hospital beds because both have fixed areas to serve customers).

In all your thinking, consider the short- and long-range ramifications of your reasoning—Who will it affect? Does it risk people's jobs? Will it hurt the organization financially? What are the consequences of it in 10 minutes, 10 months, and 10 years?

I ruminate. I mull things over. I think about it 10 times as many hours as anyone else. It looks like a reflex decision, but I've been thinking.

≈⊙≈

To manage the downside risk, I look at what's the best thing and worst thing that can happen, where either will lead in five years, and can I tolerate the worst outcome. . . . I'm more concerned about the downside risk for other people. I have 850 people reporting to me. If I mess up and get fired, it's no big deal. But if I make a decision that causes 50 people to lose their jobs, that's a very big deal.

≈⊙≈

I don't bring blank sheets of paper to meetings with my board when I'm needing to make decisions, but I do bring sheets of paper.

Make Decisions Yourself

Think about all this in the bathtub, in bed, or in church (the three places psychologists say where ideas emerge from unexpected connections).

Let go of the idea of having to have the perfect decision. Don't wait for a brilliant "Ah-ha"; just keep looking for a smart one that integrates all the information presented.

Write down your gut feeling and hunches; then put that aside just for now. Don't ignore it. Later, test it against what you ultimately do to check your initial instincts and judgment.

Don't broadcast your decision too early, especially if you're in a position of power. You can bias the helpful input of others.

Decide sooner rather than later. Holding back in decision making is worse than making a wrong decision.

Do not dwell on or overexamine the 10,000 things that *could* enter into the equation and that *could* affect the decision.

By speeding up a decision, you might take a process from a scientist's innovative dream to a product rolling off the factory line and onto retailers' shelves in six months versus two years, giving you a year and a half head start over competitors.

You get known as a go-to-get-it-done person. Better to be an aim, ready, fire person than an analysis/paralysis one.

⌘

When making decisions, people bring out an endless list of overconcerns about unintentional consequences: "If I seed the clouds, it will rain, and it might flood the rivers, and the price of corn will go up." Fact is the river may flood anyway.

⌘

I'm quick to make a decision, chose a course of action, and move forward. I don't have to review it 20 more times. Most people ponder too much. I act, and I'll make another decision later, if necessary. Tell me, how much better can more information be if I'm delayed in making the decision? Five weeks later at the deadline, people come up with a decision. If they had made it five weeks earlier, they would have had all that time to deal with the problem.

⌘

Think long. Think again. Then decide. Be patient but hurry.

If you don't a make a decision, you paralyze a whole bunch of people around you. People are largely unwilling to make decisions. They are open to new ideas when decisions are made for them—if they feel heard in the process but want to play it safe by not actually making the decisions themselves.

When you take a leap of faith and decide, you start in motion things that you could never have seen before you made the decision. And, if necessary, you can make another decision considering the new circumstances.

Meanwhile, if someone else makes a better decision, get behind it.

Sell Your Decision

It's nothing if you can't sell it. The best way to get people on board is to involve people all along in the process. Discuss, align, and engage from the start, and continue through the execution. You build trust when things are risky and full of obstacles if your people feel involved and valued. If they understand the situation and you integrate their input by at least asking questions of them before you make the decision, you'll get a "we did this" attitude instead of "our chief did this." Don't work as an island. No matter how good a decision is, if others don't buy in, contribute, help, and support, it will fail.

> *My quick or slow decisions still burden someone. If in a split-second I decide to have our company sponsor a charity event, many people, man-hours, and dollars are affected. It took me minutes to decide to sponsor an event but it can take weeks or months of planning the execution from the day, time, location, down to what brand of beer to serve. . . . Now, if some individual picks up the ball in dealing with all the ramifications of my instantaneous decision, she or he will get noticed and viewed as a valued internal leader.*

Review what happened as a result of the decision. Follow up; get empirical feedback. If it turns out that you've made a bad decision, turn on a dime to correct it.

In decision making, Murphy's law enters the picture, that being

- Anything that can go wrong will.
- Interchangeable parts won't.
- Self-starters will not.
- There's always more than one bug.
- No good deed goes unpunished.
- If you try to please everybody, nobody will like it.

> *I anticipate, expect, and am not surprised by problems. I want my people to be the same way. I tell them to defeat Murphy. That is, the worst thing will always happen at the worst time. I tell them to always expect something going wrong, anticipate what might be a likely*

scenario. They need to ask, "What could happen to mess this up?" If they don't ask that, they aren't doing the complete job. If Murphy's law didn't exist, why would I need them? So we all win if they have better ways to handle the problems I expect them to anticipate.

⋘◈⋙

Be bold to the goal, but make sure you can get there.

⋘◈⋙

As early as possible in your career, you need to get the scars of engagement and gain the judgment that goes along with them.

Review What Happened

When you review, analyze, and dissect your decisions, you learn. This is how judgment develops. The more judgment you acquire, the more you can make another call, even when information is missing, despite how much you tried to dig and get it.

Look at where you started, the steps you took, the hurdles and stumbling blocks you encountered, the changes you made to fix things, and the result or outcome. If you don't like where you ended up, think about what you'd do differently the next time, take note, and then actually refer to your notes next time.

Consider the outcome from the perspective of all involved, and repair the damage done. Do not blame others for the failure. Totally take it on yourself.

For successes, though, give credit—even more than is due—to others. Do not take credit on yourself.

Age helps. Living through up and down cycles helps. Recovering from mistakes helps. Success helps.

13

You Can Take Bad News

- Ask for it, but not *ad nauseum.*
- Take feedback with the best intent.
- Give feedback well.

TO IMPROVE, YOU NEED FEEDBACK. THERE IS NO WAY AROUND IT. A coach provides it in the athletic arena to improve a player's performance. A boss, human resources person, peer, mentor, competitor, or customer can provide it in the business arena—overtly or covertly—to improve your performance.

You can discount feedback, explain it away, deny it, ignore it, or discredit it, but you sure better seek it—and seek it out repeatedly.

It's far better to *know* than not to know what people think you do poorly or ineffectively because then you can do something about it. If you're inattentive to examination, you won't know what's holding you back.

Honest feedback can be quite painful, but "tuck your chin in and head into the storm." You need to know if they view you as "ready now" or "ready later" for more responsibility. Experts in formal leadership assessment say that successful managers look very different from their less successful peers—and that is at every level. You need to know how you stack up in your management's opinion.

If you aren't open to it and you don't seek it out, people can conclude that (1) you don't care to change and improve, (2) you are egotistical in thinking you need no improvement, (3) you are blind to reality, (4) you are satisfied with the status quo, (5) you lack ambition, and (6) you will retaliate if you get it from them.

Most people don't ask for feedback on themselves; they wait for it, half hoping that it won't come. Instead, encourage and embrace the opinions of others. If you don't encourage them, you'll hinder learning, and they may stop being attentive or caring about you.

Silence is sometimes the worst criticism because the person deems you not worth the effort to invest in.

> *Welcome criticism because then you can change, and they won't have that to use against you in the future.*

The discussion in Chapter 3 was all about constantly seeking information about your business, the business world, and the universe in general. The same need is there to constantly seek information about how you're doing but without having you be the main focus of things.

In other words, it's not because it's "all about me" that you seek feedback in a self-centered, self-focused fashion. It's about "What can I do better in my work, in my communication, in my decision making, and in my developing and helping others to do better in their work, their communication, their decision making, and their helping others do better?" This is why you seek feedback.

All feedback is not created equal. Consider the source, timing, subject and situation, recent history, past history, office politics, personality, culture, and the current business environment.

Feedback can be as much about the person giving it as about the one receiving it. Formal critique is sometimes just judging, prejudices, and biases made acceptable when put in a feedback format. It's a huge mistake to think that you are what other people say you are. Still, look for some insight that you didn't have, and view it as a positive opportunity to learn and change.

Fearing feedback is foolish. Yes, there is fraudulent feedback (stemming from political motivation), but you need to calmly and with confidence sort through that to find some nuggets for development. It's important to know what other people are thinking while still remembering that they *aren't* all-knowing.

The problem is that the more successful you are in anything, the more critiques are silenced because "you can't argue with success." Thus fewer and fewer people give feedback—formally or informally—unless you encourage it. The higher you move up in an organization, the more reluctant people are to tell you what they really think. The wealthier you become, the more you "silence, isolate, and chill people about your defects."

So brace yourself when you ask for feedback. Be prepared for more than you anticipated because it's easier and frankly more fun for people to come up with more negative observations than positive. Judging others lets them feel heard, valued, and even powerful.

"How can I make this better?" is all you need to ask. The one thing you don't want to hear from people is just your merits. Do not let friends, family, your boss, your mentor, peers, or competitors just report your virtues. You already know them because you're broadly adequate. You want to learn where to get better.

> *I accept it from everyone. Feedback is the most wonderful, powerful thing. I teach that to my four kids—that critique is just a question about something that isn't clear, isn't understood, or isn't accepted.*

> *It's a demonstration of your worth for me to be unsparing in finding fault and be sparing on flattery.*

> *People shouldn't fear feedback. We do it to test, make you strong, not kill you. We use rubber bullets here.*

> *I take cues and prompts from everything. I read, talk, have two executive coaches, get professional development experiences, take nuances from community involvement, and ask my wife how I'm doing.*

I can do something about criticism I hear, but I can't do anything about criticism I don't hear.

⋘⊛⋙

Sometimes performance opinions are fraudulent, given by frauds.

⋘⊛⋙

I cultivate multiple people for feedback all the time, strong, fundamentally irreverent individuals with no issues who will say, "I think what you're doing is off-base."

Just as you shouldn't fear mistakes, don't fear feedback. Pay attention, think, and change as you choose accordingly. It's all for learning. However, if someone provides fraudulent feedback, correct it as well.

Anything you fear takes away from your confidence. You can ignore it, discredit it, or deny it—but at least be open to hear it.

What Does Getting Frequent Feedback Mean? What Does It Look Like?

It's up to you to seek it out, and if you choose to do it (because it *is* your choice), you

- Get a heads-up when (or sometimes before) there is an issue.
- Check progress, results, and outcomes against standards of expectation.
- Check progress, results, and outcomes against your *own* expectations and goals.
- Put yourself in a position to change problem areas before problems occur.

Ask for It, but Not Ad *Nauseum*

Seek out feedback as early and frequently as possible—within reason. Anything good that is overdone becomes ineffective. If you ask too much, it looks like you're insecurely seeking approval, and people don't like to be used to pump up your ego.

At least once a year request formal feedback through objective measurement tools: assessments, appraisals, testing, colleague input, organizational psychologists, or other company-sponsored formats. To measure your progress over time, you need regular, consistent, timely, and candid comment.

Assessment inventories, tests, 360-degree feedback, and structured criteria are used to identify and promote development needs, pinpoint plateaued managers, prepare for a reorganization, dissect reasons for problem performers, and launch a professional development program to improve performance.

Formal feedback slots you into some variation of "does not meet job requirements," "overall skill set for job is on the margin," "meets job requirements," or "consider development for a larger role." People rank you among the lowest, middle, or highest levels in potential: "low performer," "inconsistent good performer," "key performer," "diamond in the rough," "rising star," or "strategic star." If you get known as a rising star, people track you from supervisor, to manager, to director, to vice president, to executive.

A report on your strengths, your development areas, and the raters' conclusions might include: "Strengths: Creative thinker who is able to articulate a compelling vision of the future and generate innovative ideas. Development areas (in communication skills, basic general management skills, internal senior-level influence, and impact): Must improve his communication skills in two areas: First, he needs to improve his ability to deliver his message in clear, concise, and simple terms. When trying to make a point, he has a tendency to go off on tangents, be verbose, to overcomplicate, and not always circle back to the original point he was intending to make. Conclusion: He demonstrates an abundance of.... however, when compared against . . . , he is relatively underdeveloped. . . . He should be considered a strong candidate in a three- to five-year time frame."

Results need to be interpreted properly and carefully with experienced judgment. Considerations such as a person's poor insight, lack of confidence, or desire to impress can alter the outcome.

Respond immediately when any of these types of feedback are offered to you. But do not limit your desire for feedback to formal evaluations. Solicit feedback in every situation.

At the least, ask human resources, "What do people think of my behavior?" "Can you come to my meetings and watch me operate?" Then ask for a debriefing. Ask the rater (e.g., boss, colleague, or mentor) to talk to your team, if they will, for more reactions.

Then work on changing based on the feedback, and in nine months do it all again.

If you work in a politically charged culture, you need to be cautious of interpretation because if someone giving feedback is loyal to a peer you have an issue with, for example, you can get skewed or false data.

Refrain from having your raters defend their comments, but do get clarification. "Tell me what you want to tell me." "Would you give me an example of when you've seen me do that?" "What would you like to see that will cause you to change your mind?" "Thank you." (Don't be looking for compliments in this exchange, by the way.)

With a pass-the-salt tone of voice and relaxed expression on your face, say, "Don't hold back. It doesn't help me." (Don't let your nostrils quiver and your lips tighten when you say this.)

Mull it over. Accept that a little self-doubt will slip in. If your response to feedback is "I don't agree," you won't learn from it. Don't cry. I know of a woman who literally lost both her contact lenses in a crying jag in her boss's office.

Don't grouse about feedback afterwards with friends over lunch or drinks or bad mouth or mimic the deliverer of the news.

Do not let it affect your health. If you want to, when it's over, do what I've heard one billionaire real estate/media mogul did. Draw the face of the person who gave you the feedback on a tennis ball, and then — play ball! (It probably would be better to put your own bad behavior on the ball and hit that around instead.)

Your objective is to find out what holds you back and do something about it. People way down in the organization, not just the chiefs around you, can provide very accurate descriptions of how you're perceived. You won't get this information without asking and without observing how people behave around you, treat you, and open up to you. Don't guess or assume something is off; ask, "How can I make this better?"

You also get feedback every day and in every way from your customers if your sales are weak, from employees if performance is slipping, from management if promotions slow down, and from outside if search consultants don't call.

If your company is losing sales to its competitor, but no one knows why, there is very little chance that the situation will change unless you find out what your customers are thinking. Likewise, if you don't know where you stand with your "customer" (e.g., management), you don't know where to go from here.

One hospital CEO initiated a program in which representatives visited patients in their homes after they were released to get the patients' experiences. While in the hospital, people felt that they couldn't complain. An early finding of this program was the need for bilingual staff because some patients couldn't understand their treatments or their follow-up instructions.

An electronics company CEO would carry a list of customers when he traveled. In between meetings, he'd phone who he could to check on their satisfaction. If there was a repair problem, he'd literally send his plane's pilot—who was cross-trained in repair—to the person's location immediately.

Only by finding out about problems can you correct them.

If you give people encouragement to identify your weaknesses, ask for their recommendations too, just as you wouldn't bring up a problem unless you also brought up a solution. Don't accept criticism without clarification on the giver's part. You deserve to know what people are using to back up their comments. If they give you the first, they must give you the second too—this goes for both formal and informal feedback.

Criticism and conflict avoidance are my favorite pastimes.

❦

Truth is, in life, you will get criticism if you aren't working hard—or if you are!

❦

At some level, you don't get criticism per se; instead, you pretty much either get vague suggestions or killed. There's not much middle ground.

❦

I rate people on a scale from 1 to 10 in competence, commitment, and confidence. That's it. That's all that counts.

Take Feedback With the Best Intent

Don't take it as a personal attack or an insult; don't think that you are flawed, unworthy, or rejected. Don't feel estranged from the person giving it, nor mistrust that person. Keep in mind that just because not everyone likes you or how you do things, you also don't have to like everyone or how they do things.

Remember, you have opinions about others, just as they do about you. Should they fear this from you? No. Nor should you fear it from them.

When your boss critiques something, you're being told what's valued in character, information, or abilities. (This is not the time to bring up his or her shortcomings—no kettle calling the pot black here.) Do nothing to cause the boss to react or he or she may say, "That's the last time I'll ever help him!"

The best thing you can do is to thank the giver of information—maybe even send a fruit basket (without sour grapes) or a handwritten note (make sure that your handwriting is legible). At the very least, say, "Well, that's interesting feedback. Thank you for that." Then say, "I'm glad you told me that" or "I appreciate you bringing that to my attention. As of this morning, I took action to change." At some later point, go out of your way to express sincere gratitude again for the person's honesty. Explain what you did to correct the situation, and tell the person the (positive) results.

One CEO told me of an incident that had happened that very morning. "I talked to a colleague and said, 'Here's a critical remark for you: You seem to have lost the ability to communicate without yelling,' whereupon she exploded and stomped out. It took courage to say it, and I really considered the wording, but I was flummoxed by the response. She could have just said, 'Thanks for the feedback.'"

Give Feedback Well

Give it on a regular basis, not sporadically—in an honest, low-key, consistent manner during the good times and the bad. Explain it to make it meaningful and relatable.

You aren't helping the person if you aren't observant or withhold information necessary for their improvement, so criticize as much as needed and praise as much as possible. Make certain not to make it into an ear bashing or a "drive-by colonoscopy," as one person put it.

Don't stall, avoid, or withhold.

One CEO told me, "I'd rather be the one criticized than the one doing the criticizing. It helps me live with fewer regrets."

Discourage bad behavior in a good way. Keep it between you two. Give the person a chance and time to change his or her behavior. Don't talk to others about the individual; talk to the individual. Give criticism directly to the person in need; if you speak to someone else about it, you are just spreading gossip. (Trashing someone behind his or her back while smiling in his or her face says more about you than about that person.)

Don't lash out emotionally, pound fists, scream, or shout. Don't insinuate, imply, insult, make a dig, peck away, or give innuendo. Great insults last a long time.

Don't let one person get away with a certain behavior and the next one not.

Think back to when you've been on the receiving end. Did you listen, appreciate, value, and change from it, or did you resent, fight, retaliate, and avenge? It likely depends on how the feedback was given.

One young manager told me this story: "My boss called me into the boardroom and pulled out two chairs from the table so that we would face each other. She sat down in her Prada pants suit, legs spread, hands on her knees, elbows out, hunched shoulders, and bored into my eyes and peeled my face off with seething critique. Right then she sealed the keg as to not getting support from me in the future. It just will never happen."

"I do everything I can to make sure that I don't batter, bruise, or bloody the person."

Spend as much time in recognition and praise as in criticism. (Studies show that marriages last longer if for every negative interchange, there are five positive ones.) People at all levels crave praise. It makes people feel that their hard work isn't in vain. So give praise—even if you have to do like one CEO told me, "I schedule in praise on my calendar."

The best feedback you can give to others is noticing something positive about the person and saying it out loud to the person or to someone else who will likely tell the person.

Address behavior, not character or motives. Maintain the person's self-esteem while you address limiting behavior that is offensive. "Your presentation needs improvement in . . ." is different from "You always disappoint me in your presentations, and I feel that you don't care."

If you don't change after hearing feedback, people will conclude that you don't (1) listen and learn, (2) believe and trust their opinion, and (3) care about their judgment. They will cease caring about you and providing you with feedback and will put their effort into someone who is interested. If you refuse to change, at least surround yourself with people who make up for your weaknesses.

Get feedback. Get suggestions to improve. Try a suggestion. Get feedback if that resulted in an improvement. Then add additional suggested improvements or tips, check the results, and continue the cycle.

When you work with noble intent, intense focus and effort, and your spirits are lifted with your results, do not look to others for approval or appreciation. Your own judgment outweighs theirs.

14

You Are Willing to Make Mistakes

- Get into setbacks early on.
- Admit mistakes and fix them.
- Keep going.

MAKING MISTAKES PROVES THAT YOU'RE DOING SOMETHING. Good for you. Gain from them, apply what you learned, don't repeat them, and don't stop trying harder. Let others make mistakes too so that they can learn also.

> I don't care if people make mistakes. I only care about what they learned. Everybody, everyday makes mistakes or at least is imperfect. If they avoid them, no one learns anything, and it causes everybody to be afraid to admit what they did.

> I forgive them immediately and remind them of four or five things they did well. My mentor taught me to reinforce the positive and deemphasize the negative.

Employees who mess up are ultimately better employees because they had a second chance ... like getting a dog from the pound.

Early on in your career, mistakes feel like a big deal. They are seldom a big deal. The quarterback doesn't sit on the bench after a bad throw, does he? No, he gets out and runs another pass. Instead of thinking you need a machine to kick your own butt, go throw a touchdown.

Almost all mistakes *are forgivable.*

You'll learn more from one bad decision than all the good ones you'll ever make. One study found that you master the same from two mistakes that you acquire from 20 successes. Now, this shouldn't be your primary method of acquiring knowledge, of course.

Confident people see slip-ups as a badge of honor and admit mistakes right away. And they prefer to be around others who've survived misfortunes of their own.

Almost all mistakes are forgivable—well, except things like the *Exxon Valdez.* Hopefully, yours are never at that level. There are degrees of mistakes. I'm writing about the everyday type we all make, not malfeasance.

If you are in a boat you can't plug, then you better seek counsel for your decision. Know when to bring the superior officer in. Don't sink the boat.

I'm not taking lightly mistakes that cause loss of life, limb, or property or demonstrate that you aren't doing your job. Those are major issues and errors that have to be avoided and should be feared. You and I don't deal with those daily, though. Our slip-ups are typos, lapses of memory, presentation stumbles, missed deadlines, misrepresentations, misinterpretations, and so forth. Few slips-ups have results like comedian Phyllis Diller's comment: "What I don't like about the office Christmas party is looking for a job the next day."

Truth be told, a very visible, very public, very costly mistake is not acceptable. Sometimes you do get fired.

If you stumble a multiple of times, it results in more challenging dialogue.

The same mistake twice is a different conversation.

I'm *not* promoting mistakes; the fewer there are in life, the better it is for all of us. I *am* promoting action—taking the lead and making decisions despite being afraid of what might go wrong. Nothing gets done at all if you wait to do it so well that no one can find any fault with it. Being faint-hearted will inhibit you from starting your long line of successes if you let it. As a leader, you have to rationalize away all the red flags and go for it.

Fearing failure, that is, risk aversion, is much more of a career killer than making mistakes.

Have humility. Swallow your pride. Take your licks. Get knocked down. And pick yourself up and start all over again. Don't throw in the towel when the work slaps you up aside the head.

If you don't make a mistake, you start getting a trust-fund-baby mentality. If you don't work and worry your way through it, you don't appreciate the good or the bad.

Speed bumps are inevitable. You can doubt yourself every single day. We all do. When you're in a painful situation and it's really tough, let your look of fear come out as a look of confidence.

Lose the fear ... lose the groupthink ... lose the yes-people ... lose the chain of command ... lose the consultants ... lose the focus groups ... lose the safety nets ... lose consensus ... lose the happy medium ... lose the compromises ... lose Plan B. ... Keep the drive.

—From a BMW automobile advertisement

Most people are raised not to make mistakes. We have a culture of avoiding them. The question is, How do you learn from them if you avoid them? What's even worse is an environment where you spend more effort covering up mistakes than admitting them, learning from them, and moving on.

The biggest mistake is not to persevere. A line in the movie *Rocky V* (which I'm sure you all have seen) says it well: "Life will beat you down and pound you. The beating is *not* about how hard you can hit but can be hit." You must maintain your ambition even after setbacks.

It's okay to err, and err, and err (appropriate to your level) as long as it's in different areas and you do it less, and less, and less and you walk away with new knowledge. The career killers are not learning from mistakes and being one to deny, shirk, or point fingers.

The biggest killer of talent is getting kicked in the teeth a couple of times and you decide, "I'm done."

If you want something you've never had, you have to do something you've never done.

Unless you take a chance, you may never know what you're missing out on. And neither will the rest of the world.

Take risks, but not stupid ones.

It's impossible to live without failure unless you live so cautiously that you fail by default.

When the Professional Rodeo Cowboys Association (PRCA) was founded, it was originally named the Cowboy Turtle Association (CTA) because the cowboy members had to stick their neck out to make progress. We could start something today called the Leader Turtle Association (LTA) because you have to do the same thing. If you don't "stick your neck out," when you are sitting on your porch swing at age 84, you're going to want to kick yourself for not having done so.

Now, if you make incorrect decisions that lead to mistakes because you (1) lack information, (2) have no desire to find the correct information, and (3) don't care, then you made a mistake in buying this book too.

It's normal and natural to have some trepidation about making a blunder. You can be scared, but you must go forth and try anyway. Once past the racing heart, trembling, lightheadedness, nausea, difficulty breathing, sweating, and fear of doing something embarrassing, you must realize that it's okay to persevere.

What Does Being Willing to Make a Mistake Mean? What Does It Look Like?

If you choose to do this (because it *is* your choice), you

- Know the mistake is seldom permanent.
- Know that no one will remember it as long as you do.
- Learn that the rest of the world is more important than you.
- Build character.
- Keep your ego in check.
- Humble yourself.
- Show that you're willing to stumble and learn from it.
- Get noticed.

Get into Setbacks Early On

You'll have more time for a better chance of recovery and get comfortable with your "stupidity" early on, and you'll come to know important things sooner. One chief told me, "My new boss and I were walking out of the building together to go to lunch. He grabbed me by my collar and pushed my back up against the wall so hard and for so long that I thought I'd get third-degree burns from the hot wall in the afternoon sun. He held me there and said, 'Get in trouble as fast as you can.'"

I really don't want you to succeed too early or too often. You'll get lazy, lose your edge, get sloppy, and end up making more mistakes.

The worst time for failure is 20 years down the road into your career, when you fall flat on your face for the first time and don't know how to recover.

Let others around you get into mistakes early too so that you learn how they handle themselves and they learn from the experience.

When you have a setback, it's life. When you learn to walk, you fall a lot—just stand on your feet and walk again.

Young people are petrified to fail because they were so nurtured by their parents. They get to the edge of the water but are afraid to wade in. They want a safe path across.

Missteps, mistakes, and failures will occur. Good for you. That's how you grow. If you're lucky, you'll run into speed bumps every day. Be prepared for bumps and bruises; scar up a little from the start.

Don't make the same mistake over and over. If you do something that doesn't work, don't do it again. You get one ticket per issue. Now, this is true "unless it's really a fun mistake," as one CEO advised: "Then you might want to do it more than once." (Apparently, this is not necessarily a recommendation in tennis: A British study found that 44 percent of line judge calls are wrong.)

Don't go small; go big. When you decide to take a gamble, double the risk first. Act like you know what you are doing, stick to it, and give it plenty of oomph. It looks less foolish to lose big than small. One female CEO in a public relations and advertising company proudly stated that she liked to make the biggest mistake possible to get noticed by men.

Prepare for missteps every time you take risks. No path is without cost. Missteps will happen even with good outcomes.

Recover, get back on track, even leverage them.

I closed a deal that turned out well. It was a risk I was willing to take, even though the company was not. I went ahead and did it, and it

was a success. Others with a different risk tolerance were envious of my outcome and labeled me as a renegade, a cowboy who got lucky. They were jealous of my success.

Admit the Mistakes and Fix Them

Everyone makes mistakes; not everyone lives up to them. (It shows character either way you choose to take.) Embrace the mistake by privately analyzing how it happened and maybe even publicly explaining the circumstances. It's all about how you deal with it.

Apologize (if appropriate). Don't overapologize; it weakens you, displays insecurity, begs for affirmation, and makes the other person compelled to make you feel good by saying, "Oh no, it's not that bad." Overdoing anything takes away its effectiveness and just gives your competitors something to rally around.

Recognize, correct, and don't repeat. Talk about your mistakes in a free and open exchange to diminish any additional fallout.

If you make a mistake, don't make it permanent. Fix it.

When things don't turn out the way you wanted, I say, "That's okay. Now tell me what you learned." Sometimes I promote mistakes just so people have the opportunity to learn. It's also a way to root out dishonest ones—those who won't admit mistakes. Because people who don't make mistakes are lying—they are just covering up the ones they made.

On average, only 2 out of 10 projects I work on result in a home run.

Privately analyze a mistake yourself to avoid repeating it: "What were the cycle of events that led up to it?" "Where did I fail to prepare?" "What ability/skill did I lack?" "When did I sense a problem?" "What did or didn't I do and should have?" "How will I handle this differently in the future?"

On the major networks, new series come out every fall. The industry standard is 10 failures for every one success. So the network executives study the flop and ask, "Why did viewers not like . . . ? Why did they like . . . ? Why did we fail?"

Suzy Welch says that when she was the editor of the *Harvard Business Review*, every week every editor had to phone a subscriber who canceled and find out why.

A Harvard Divinity School student who loudly booed at a President Bush speech and was arrested for disorderly conduct, jailed for the night, and then fined, says, "If there's one thing I learned, it's that if you want to interrupt the president of the most powerful nation in the world while he's delivering his inaugural address, it's going to cost you about $25."

View every mistake you make as a new adventure. Then fix it. All people make mistakes. The good leader knows when he or she is wrong and immediately repairs the damage.

One CEO told me that "a rant from a customer was a gift from God" because it made me aware and motivated me to do something about it quickly.

Your mistake is a failure if you don't understand how and why it happened and what to do about it. Console yourself that the compensation for an error is education.

Keep Going

After you've learned what you can from your mistake, forget the mistake, but remember the learning. Do the "time" (hopefully *not* jail time) and even be willing to quit the job if it will help the situation.

Don't fret. Do your best. Move on.

Don't let a mistake affect you for the future — only at this point in time. Be lightly and temporarily angry mainly at yourself. Within 24 hours, get back in the saddle in some productive, constructive, and visible task.

Failure is almost always temporary. Tomorrow is a new day.

Don't worry; in 100 years you'll be dead.

When I asked one CEO about mistakes he's made, he paused and really struggled with an answer about whether he'd made any. "I'm sure I have, I guess. But I've never assessed it. I just keep moving. Now, as you get me thinking about it, things have gone wrong, like my intent not accomplished, cost overruns, projects not completed on schedule. But I just did my mea culpas, fessed up, and made sure everyone knew I learned from it. I viewed it as an opportunity to build trust and confidence in my people by my willingness to improve from it."

Work so hard and courageously that it is inevitable that you'll make mistakes. Never hide them. Always admit, correct, fix, and then keep going. Encourage others above, alongside, and below you to do the same. This is how the entire organization gets better and moves forward.

15

You Manage Your Career and Don't Let Others Do It

- What to do if you don't get the promotion or move.
- As you evaluate moves, evaluate bosses.
- Be the boss of your career.

YOU, NOT YOUR BOSS, HUMAN RESOURCES, A SPONSOR, your parents, or search firms control and are responsible for your career. The biggest, costliest, and most avoidable mistake you can make in your life is not managing your own destiny from the start—and continuing throughout.

This sounds easier said than done, I know. Still, if your lifework is not determined by you, it will be by someone else—someone who knows and cares a lot less than you do about your ability, drive, and potential.

> *I always had good options presented to me, yet my biggest regret is too much going with the flow. I wish I had taken control of my career sooner.*

181

The downside of you managing your career is that you don't know where to go and don't have the talent, but you take control anyway and drive it into a brick wall.

When I track the careers of CEOs I have interviewed, I can accurately and emphatically state that (if you're on a leadership track) every 2.5 years you need to have advanced yourself with a move to a broader role with more complex work responsibility and stepped-up risk—a bigger job, a growth area, additional duties, stretch assignments, a larger budget, extra people, a chance to be in charge, a bigger subgroup, or a combination of the preceding.

You manage this by first being objectively aware of where you are, what you've done, what you can do, and where you should go next.

How do you find this out? With communication, observation, and constantly acquiring knowledge from your feedback sources (e.g., boss, mentor, peers, competitors, and circle of contacts).

You commit to yourself and learn all you can about your current job so that you can justifiably move on. You meet company goals and exceed the company's expectations, but more important, you meet your own goals and exceed your own expectations—fostering an environment for others below and above to do the same.

Then you let people know that it's time for you to move up and/or move on. Do not make change for money alone. Make change if you've learned all you can.

Do not make job changes just for more money. That is not the point, and it would be a mistake to do it for that reason alone. The first five or six job changes are about learning and getting the opportunity to show what you're made of. If you prove you do exceptional work, people will be fighting to have you and begging you to take their money. All you have to say is "Okay." Good leaders are quickly identified, and they never have to ask for more money. Jobs and money find them.

Get an appetite for the journey because you'll never know where you're going.

Choose a route with many twists and turns.

Go in to your boss and tell him what you want to do in your career. Don't ask where he thinks you should go. Say, "I take responsibility for my career. I want to eventually run the place. I have mentors who give me advice. I constantly study and learn about my specialty, my industry, and business in general. I'm volunteering for any grunt work you want done. I'll clean up the urinal if it needs it. I'll do anything everyone else doesn't want to do, and I'll do it over and over." ... In my 21 years of running the show, no one has ever done this with me. If they did, they'd be halfway to their goal.

When the ability to acquire new knowledge starts to flatten out, change positions.

Don't leave until you've gotten all you can out of it. In other words, if you think you've learned all you can learn and it's now a dead end, then leave. But don't leave before you've got the benefit of the experience. Some people jump around just because of the money and don't get the learning of how to really progress. So don't leave too soon.

Don't allow yourself to be moved around solely for the company's benefit but do what's right for you too. Information you know only if you've thought about it along with the benefit of getting other's thinking.

Don't wait for the company to give you increased duty. You have to create your own breakthrough role. Find yourself a new assignment; do a gap analysis of what it takes and what you have; do something about the gap; and on your own initiative, persuasively go after the job goal. Opportunities you go to in your career are the most rewarding ones; responsibility handed to you isn't as rewarding and frankly often has something the matter with it.

I had to learn how to run a business entirely on my own, no mentor, no support. I was with an organization that wanted to start a Denver office, but none of the partners wanted to go, so I said, "Send me," because they said they'd give support. But it turns out they didn't. I learned business the way soldiers learn geography, by crawling over every inch of it.

With the need for speed in business leadership, companies can't drag their feet in promoting, and you can't be so easygoing in taking on more.

You decide where you want to go—and go for it—rather than just drifting. (There's a lot of drifting going on.) Those who think about it and plan for it (even a little) do a lot better. The odds are stacked against you unless you do. It's easy to be passive; that why it's so popular.

Plan, but don't plan on your plan working out because there is no way you can anticipate the myriad changes, surprises, and setbacks you'll encounter. You'll end up in jobs, companies, and industries you haven't even considered. You'll change; the world will change. The one thing that can remain the same is your sustained effort to learn all you can and then move on.

If you don't have butterflies starting your new job, you're not reaching.

The best professional development tool is a big job. You've got to try stuff that on paper you have no right to but that seems like a good idea anyway. Some of the new big jobs won't work out flawlessly, but if you win all the time, it means you aren't competing at a high enough level.

As you progress from supervisor to manager to director to vice president to C-level executive, as much as possible, go after jobs that you'd do whether you were paid or not. When you choose jobs or assignments, do it to develop, enhance, and complete the picture.

I never took a job that didn't interest me. To make sure, I never interviewed for a job that I didn't want.

I've been in sales, finance, brand management. I like to say I have a career I wouldn't wish on anyone but wouldn't change for anything.

I did learn what I liked and didn't like. It was the process of distillation that led to the perfect job.

You, not human resources, your boss, a sponsor, your parents, or search firms, control your career. Objectively look at where you are, what you've done, what you still can do, and where you could go—*then do what you should next*—and continue. Ask and deserve promotions. Simultaneously sponsor others in their efforts.

Don't move just because you have a situation you can't fix. But don't wait until something really attractive comes along either. If you cling to a job because it's comfortable, the commute is easy, your in-laws are close, you love the company or the people, you have no desire to change, you lack focus, you lack confidence, and you can do it with your eyes closed, you're making a career blunder.

What Does Managing Your Career Mean? What Does It Look Like?

If you choose to do this (because it *is* your choice), you

- Are willing to work for a boss you don't like and still make the boss look good and smart.
- Learn how people get promoted in your organization and do the same and more.
- Help your boss get promoted and help your subordinates get promoted.
- Consistently exceed your own expectations and even do better than others think you will.
- Take it on yourself to learn how profit and loss happens in your organization.
- Solve problems and make issues go away and communicate so that others know what your team has accomplished and the value they add to the organization.
- Coach your people on the next steps they should take after each of their accomplishments.

- Get a replacement ready to take your place.
- Look, work, walk, and talk (without a hint of arrogance) like you are already in the next job before you are so that people "see" you in it.

Decide What You Need and Want to Do Next

Sit and think what you'd like to do next. Whether you are a supervisor, manager, director, vice president, or executive, think about and write a list of what *you* want — not just what they want or value — in professional development, personal growth, location/lifestyle, compensation, and other things important to you. List them, rank them on a scale of 1 to 10, and then when you are considering a move, you can test what you feel about the new opportunity against your objective ranking. Seek ideas and information on the possibilities by reading and talking to your network of contacts, mentors, and spouse. Study and lay out options.

> *Go to the boss's boss and say, "I'd like to buy you lunch" or "Can I have 10 minutes of your time ... because I'd like to understand...." Always tell them how much time you'll take because we don't want to commit to unended time.*

Find out top management's interests or the CEO's pet project, if possible. Ask your boss what's needed most, what would add the biggest value to the company regardless of whether it's in line with your specialty or not. Talk to human resources about what they see as next steps. Poll search consultants about what good options are. If you talk to a lot of people (while at the same time continuing to peruse printed material), you'll get a point of valuable information here and here and there.

Find and talk to people (inside and outside your company) already doing the jobs that you are interested in pursuing, and go and talk to them about the work — the challenges, opportunities, frustrations, and obstacles — and observe them for a day, if possible. (Your interest likely will increase their self-esteem. Think about how you'd feel if some up-and-comer wanted to follow you around.) Take your own personal time if necessary. You also may want to speak to people who chose not to take the job to get their reasoning for turning it down.

Put all the points of intelligence together, and set your course.

Don't call me and offer yourself as the solution to my problems without knowing the situation.

Be able to give a 30- to 40-second verbal rendition of the void that needs to be filled, the benefit to the company, and why you're the person to do it because of your

1. Background, experience, training, education, and/or achievements
2. Job skills, business acumen, and company and customer knowledge
3. Competencies and values in managing, communicating to, and leading others

If you ask for a role change, after you make a case for it, the person might say, "Okay." If he or she doesn't, at least the person knows that you want it.

I had cases in the basement filled with awards as engineer of the year, manager of the year, and so on. Even though I had demonstrated performance, I had to ask for a promotion. I gave them two choices so that I didn't box them in, but they were unaware I wanted to move up.

Companies do not really have loyalty to employees. They want employees to be extremely loyal, but you can't count on the company to take care of you as an individual. You must constantly be considering yourself as your own business; promote and take care of yourself because the company will not.... marry your skill set; don't marry your company.

I got the CEO job when I was 8½ months pregnant. The company I was with was looking for a CEO, and I said, "What about me?" I believe if you leap, the net will appear.

Your first and second requests might have to be followed up with action, such as the action this man took: "Not only did I tell the person with the decision-making power, but I told lots of people above him who also told him about my interest. I made a point to sit next to my potential new boss at a managers' meeting, expressed my desire, and outlined my qualifications."

As with anything good, taken to the extreme, this can be bad. One small division president got promoted after months of excessive lobbying for a bigger group. He kept pressuring the CEO and the board to the point that to avoid losing him, they gave him the presidency of an $800 million division. Three months later the job they were grooming him for but couldn't explain to him at the time came open—that being the president of a $1.5 billion division. Had he been patient, the bigger job would have been his.

At least, if you plant the idea and initiate effort, you might get something approved before the standard human resources guideline and timeline. But be ready for rejection too.

What to Do If You Don't Get the Promotion or Move

Handle the disappointment well. Congratulate the person who got the job, and tell him or her that you'll be supportive, that you'll help the person succeed in the new role. Senior management will be watching how you handle the situation as much as watching the person who got the nod.

Turn up your personal development as well as work/results effort where needed. To find out, solicit feedback from people who will give you the truth. Don't be defensive; find out if it was a skill gap or fit gap. Change, improve, and when available, try for another promotion or move.

In the meantime, accept the seemingly unacceptable *for now*. For now, accept it, breathe, pause, relax, rethink, turn up your effort, and then try again later. You have to be adaptable and go with the flow even when it's going against you. Sometimes, for a time, "you have to take flak from idiots." Work collaboratively (for now) with people you don't like. You're being watched as much for what you do as for how you do it in a less than perfect situation.

Do not decide to leave the company as your first reaction. You'll know it's time to leave when "the smell of the place changes," meaning that you just know, deep in your gut, and it's for goal-achieving not tension-relieving reasons.

Talk to your boss. Find out his or her pet projects, and get involved in those. Few bosses will demote someone who is working on a favorite project. Simultaneously, get off any project the boss doesn't like.

Initiate cost reductions in your department. Don't pressure the boss for an expanded budget — instead, ask for a leaner, tighter budget.

Tell your boss that you know that times are tough and that you are willing to accept and promote an across-the-board pay cut.

Volunteer for additional duties. Find a vacuum, and fill it. Show your crossover ability. You'll become too valuable to lose. Improve your relations with other departments; this is no time for empire building.

Maintain a positive, cooperative attitude — it takes pressure off the boss, and you won't appear like a malcontent. Likewise, maintain a sense of humor — and keep away from negative people and conversations.

Have the guts to make decisions. If you appear scared and timid, you decrease others' confidence in you. Have the guts also to ask more questions. Don't allow ambiguity. Miscommunication gives people an excuse to dismiss you.

Show implicit trust that your boss will figure a way out of the situation and that you can help be part of the solution. Work on increasing others' trust in you — make sure that people aren't nervous around you.

Come in early, and stay late (a little more than usual). Get out of the carpool, if necessary, so that you aren't tied to leaving at 5:01.

Have a mental plan B; that is, "If I don't get the next promotion, I'll take steps 1, 2, and 3." The mental preparation will relax you and improve your performance. Care, but don't care too much about keeping this job. Remember, desperate-looking people are not wanted.

Now, if in addition to the promotion refusal there is a material reduction in the nature of your duties or the scope of your responsibility without your consent or a reduction of your base salary compared with what was in effect on your start date (unless there is an across-the-board proportionate reduction in salaries), or the company is requiring you to be based somewhere farther than within 50 miles of the company office you're hired in, it might be a sign that the smell of the place is changing.

And finally, place the e-mail or letter that notified you of the rejection news on a gravel road and drive back and forth over it several times.

It goes without saying, but I will say it anyway, you had better have done exemplary work in your current role before taking on another. You had to be productive and valuable, and you had to help your coworkers be productive and valuable.

As it relates to your current job, you have to be the one who books sales, produces outcomes, grows the department, or takes on a troubled project—whatever mission you have, you accomplish it yourself and cause others to be similarly effective. When you and your people meet the short-, intermediate-, and long-term goals and objectives in your job description and your company's mission statement, you will have enormous power. One CEO said, "I will put up with a lot of nonsense if they accomplish their goals."

If you are effective personally but not with your coworkers, you will not move up far or fast. One CEO said, "I have a long history of firing the top sales person and have sales go up. The same is true in engineering and finance. You can't be a star and eat your young."

Two groups I met with while writing this book were high-level managers from a collection of companies. The first group all shared having been promoted recently (group A). The second group all had been passed over recently for a promotion (group B). I asked individuals in both groups to explain how it happened in their own words.

Group A—recently promoted: "What I did":

- I took an assignment no one wanted and nailed it.... I committed to a senior customer to get a large project done in an extremely short period of time and then delivered it ahead of that time.
- I performed consistently well at a higher level (two levels above) while taking on challenging, high-risk assignments.
- I supported my boss.
- Right time and place.

- No one thing: consistent performance, maintained improvement, respect of others, willingness to change.
- When I missed a job promotion I turned up more passion; they saw it, and I got a better promotion six months later.
- I brought a troubled program in on target.
- I returned to work after three maternity leaves. My husband believes each baby got me a promotion.
- Mentoring relationship.
- Dearth of experience: individual contributor, first-line leader, engineer, systems integration, etc.
- I pointed out my accomplishments to my boss and provided justification for why I should be promoted.
- Being honest; being authentic.
- I brought passion and positive attitude to every job.
- I took chances: I volunteered in a teaching assistant job for the president that helped me build a network with executives, and I made a career choice that was not a good fit but a great learning experience.
- I worked for great people.
- I took a break and moved overseas. Got out of my comfort zone. Changed jobs in different locations: found a place in a completely unrelated area where almost nobody knew me.
- I led a large organization through change and to improved, sustained performance in the corporation.

Group B—recently passed over for promotion: "The person who got the job had . . ."

- Boldness, confidence, courage; he didn't care what others said, . . . took a chance without worrying about his education level, . . . took himself less seriously than I.
- The opportunity to present to senior management—I saw it, and it was good—so he got the job.
- The willingness to sacrifice and relocate.
- Different experience, superior intelligence. Technical competence. A good story. Diverse experience base.

- Connections, political skills, and a good ole boy. The person managed his career, had a powerful sponsor, a champion. He had social skills. Had spent time as an intern and had strong relationships with management.
- Drive. She established milestones for each year that built to the next job. Focused on goals; managed her perceptions.
- Gave acceptance to others instead of being impatient with others.

As You Evaluate Moves, Evaluate Bosses

Pick good bosses. You can learn from a good or a bad boss; you just learn different things in different ways.

You want a boss who will pat you on the back in public and kick you in the butt behind closed doors.

I determined, from watching the CEO, that this is how I will never run a company.

You don't always have a choice, of course. But when you look at a company to work for, look for the right boss in that company. How do you know? You talk with people who might know through your contacts and mentors.

You can do the same things that executive search firms do to find candidates and centers of influence. They ask people who's the best and brightest, they research them in the industry and business press, they initiate contact to develop a relationship, and they maintain the association.

Don't work for stupid people because they'll bring you down with them.

How do you know a good boss? He or she is a template for the information presented in this book. He or she

- Feels broadly adequate.
- Has unquestionable integrity.
- Sets and meets goals.

- Gets promoted faster than his or her peers.
- Invests in you and coaches, trains, and mentors.
- Will just as quickly give you a "pat on the back" as a "kick in the butt."
- Will actively sponsor you.
- Constantly communicates.
- Is visible.
- Has work/life balance, and understands, supports, and pushes you to have it too.
- Has worldly awareness.
- Isn't jealous of you and won't hold you back.
- Doesn't worry about "covering his or her rear."
- Has good people skills and is liked, trusted, memorable, impressive, credible, comfortable, and charismatic.
- Has professional demeanor.
- Is decisive.
- Has great processes to learn from.
- Understands work politics.
- Thinks before talking.
- Doesn't fear making mistakes.
- Asks lots of questions.
- Wants to see you successful.

My boss would always provide cover for me if I needed it.

My boss would drop everything no matter what kind of meeting he's in and get back to me on the phone within five minutes.

I was a junior guy, and I made a decision—a very bad decision. My boss got called on it in a board meeting in front of everybody. "How could you let this happen?" they demanded. He said, "I screwed up." He took the heat for my mistake right there, and I'll never forget that. That's a good boss. I learned a lot from him.

I knew I could do the job, and I finally got to prove it. I had an incredible boss who gave me a chance to verify myself. He sent me to Germany to represent him. I was in a meeting, questioning the CEO, and I myself was only one step above an administrative assistant.

My manager kept a list of people he watched who don't report to him, but he'd try to work their career path. "Can we agree to make this person available for a different opportunity?" he'd ask the person's boss. They'd say, "We're thinking about it." So he'd say, "I'll take that as a yes." And he'd follow up in six months to make sure something had happened.

The higher up the corporate ladder, the more retained headhunters are used to recruit senior executives. *Retained* means that the firm is paid in advance to search for candidates as opposed to contingency employment agencies, which are paid only after they find and place (usually) lower-level candidates.

Fifty percent of CEO searches are done using search firms (progressively less as you go down the ranking). The larger firms have the resources to compare levels of quality and excellence in thinking capabilities and problem solving, leadership and interpersonal skills, emotion and motivation, influence, etc. between North American, Latin America, or northern and western European executives. They have competitive pay assessment tools and special pay arrangements (e.g., employment contracts, severance, change-of-control programs, corporate events such as IPOs, spin-offs, mergers and acquisitions, and joint ventures) and special retention programs. They have performance measurement standards in selection, goal setting, pay for performance, and shareholder expectations.

To fit a "best in class" profile, you are viewed as more recruitable by search firms if you've been in a classic and respected blue-chip company, leave for a few years to join a McKinsey & Company or Bain to gain strategic thinking and lots of business and industry exposure, and then return to an industry with a major international business.

It also helps in your profile if you were accepted into a good school, got great academic grades, earned an MBA, had internships at Fortune 500 companies, speak two languages, traveled widely, had parents who were both executives at Fortune 500 companies, and two of your siblings work at big companies.

In addition, it also helps in your profile if you are a proven performer and had multiple assignments in more than one function, line of business, and geographic area. And you've worked in other companies, had international experience, make a positive impression, are well known by senior management, are willing to move anywhere, and are poised for more. Then your potential is pretty high to be recruited by a search firm.

They do not try to find you a job (they are not your friend, only professionally friendly); they try to find the ideal candidate for their paying client. If they think you might have the exact requirements for the position or know someone who does, they will contact you. They almost always know of you before you know they are looking at you. They solve their needs, not yours, on their timetable. So don't think keeping them on speed dial will get you into a new role.

There are good ones and not-so-good ones, as in any profession.

We see the good candidates before they even know they're being watched.

We sometimes initiate a silent search where no calls are made, but a year in advance we've started working with a search firm.

Make sure that your assistant doesn't screen their calls. Instead, have him or her convey a helpful attitude and put them through to your voice mail—as he or she would for your mentor, boss, or subordinate. Be a source of ideas, contacts, and introductions when they call or when you meet someone that might be of interest to them. Don't plan on contacting them only when you're looking for a job. First, it's not their role to find you a job. Second, they want to hear about you from others, not you.

Third, it's about the least effective thing you can do with them. And finally, still, it's worth a small shot to put your résumé onto their online file.

I get a call everyday from a recruiter. It comes from my networking.

I say "No" a lot. I think they like that. I give them help since I know lots of people. If they want to interview me, I tell them, "I'm too old to interview [she's 47]. I'll just have lunch." I think everything they tell you in the little book on job hunting you should do the opposite.

Always have a will and a résumé.

Take on the New Role

One of the best things about a new job, project, assignment, etc. is that you can go in however you want, and people accept you as you present yourself. Now's the time to seriously heed feedback from previous situations and make changes going in so that the new people do not see the old you—only the new, improved you.

Respect the organization you are going into. Don't act like a know-it-all coming in from the outside. Don't judge them or the way they do things or compare them to how you've done things.

Get in early and stay late (occasionally). Pay attention to your appearance, demeanor, and comportment. Get out and among people early and often. Greet everyone from receptionists to the CEO with eye contact and a smile. (All levels are watching, and all can help or hurt you in the future.)

Learn the care and feeding of your boss. Get a shared definition of the job by you and your boss. Establish what the realistic, company-committed important issues are, and establish metrics to evaluate progress. Document accomplishments. Fully appreciate the magnitude of the challenge and the realism of the goal and the latitude, freedom, and resources available to you to make decisions within an agreed-on timetable.

Have your own vision of where you see the job going—the future potential. Bring in your own ideas. Think through and prioritize the work you need to do and the goals you need to set and share—for the first week, month, and 90 days.

Get acquainted with the political environment so that you are familiar with who the influencers, alliances, and coalitions are in the power structure. Learn how it's done here—priorities, people, communication, meetings, etc. Ask whose support you'll need, what do they want out of this, and what has worked well in the past. Find out who drives things here, what the agendas and hidden agendas are, and what the motives and abilities of the people are. Find out if people cooperate when they work as a team and when they don't. Learn the norms, habits, and history that likely will affect your success. Observe what needs to be repaired or healed in the organization.

Ask plenty of questions, and write down what you learn. Be aware that some people will help you but that others will trick you and test you—maybe because they are jealous that you got the job. Don't rely on what others say or report about people, product, team, goals, plans, etc. Find out for yourself.

Establish and fully disclose your management and leadership style, and then be consistent in executing with everyone in every circumstance. *Do not* be one way to one group and another way to another group.

Pay dues all over again. Meet deadlines. Do grunt work in full view. Jump on opportunities to make tough decisions. Take a strong stand from time to time.

Try to break through old cliques, and don't succumb to supporting or joining one—be your own person.

Establish your system of communication. Grasp their system: Find out what was there, and speak clearly as to changes, if necessary. Make it easy for people to learn who you are; self-disclose. Then repeat and repeat to let them know your management and leadership style, family, interests, etc.

People pick apart what you say. I approached a group of them talking after a meeting and I asked what they were doing. "Trying to figure out what you need." I just told you what I need. Did you hear what I said? "Yeah, but we're trying to figure out what you need." Just ask me, I'm right here.

Do some good stuff really soon, such as chair a task force, volunteer for a project (particularly an undesirable one), turn around a situation, fix a significant people demand, start up something major, or manage a crisis.

If in your new job your boss is younger than you,

- Get fit. You look and feel younger and more energetic if you exercise, eat right, and stay in shape.
- Stand tall. Hunched and slouched looks old and lazy.
- Make fewer mistakes. You're supposed to know better; you don't have the youthful freedom to mess things up.
- Look happy. Keep a relaxed, affable expression. A frown or scowl makes you look intimidated; a smile makes the wrinkles go up instead of down. And while at it, be nice. Crotchety is old.
- Keep current in technology, music, and general trends. You don't have to like the new stuff; you just need to know about it.
- Dress modern enough. Don't wear your favorite outfit that's carried you through three U.S. presidents' terms. Your clothes don't have to be trendy, but they shouldn't be dowdy either. People notice your clothes even if theirs aren't so spiffy. One stodgy older executive had the audacity in this day and age to talk about a female executive who wore a pants suit saying she was "too lazy to put on panty hose and wear a skirt."
- Refrain from saying, "When I was young...."

Work as if you own the company from day one. Fight like it's your own; be your own boss. Roll up your sleeves and engage enthusiastically. Take ownership in the workings of the company by constantly asking, "How does this work? How do we make money? Where is more money to be made? What are the gains?" And then connect the dots.

Keep your inherited team long enough to sort out the good from the not-so-good. Decide who should be moved up or out. Take appropriate action.

By the six-month mark, you need to have some wins that improved productivity, increased sales, or something that added value. Exceed expectations.

Do not spend time fighting over a better corner office, new furniture in the office, or other signs that you've arrived.

> *I always needed effective people more than I had effective people who needed to be noticed. I had to settle for lame lots of times.*

Understand the Role of Human Resources in Your Career

If you look at them as a value-added partner, trust their expertise, champion their initiatives, and don't just come to them when you need them, human resources will do you no harm. Human resources, handled well, in conjunction with senior management, aid in your career progression internally. You still need to be at the helm of the activity, whether dealing with human resources inside or outside your organization.

They are just people like you, human, compassionate, and typically driven by fairness, but they have to follow the rules and regulations of the company and adhere to state and federal guidelines. Their goal is to get the best from their employees. If you buck the system the way the company needs to achieve results, you create a problem for them and therefore for yourself.

> *We are not the breeding ground for monsters [spoken by a human resources executive].*

So be very nice to human resources. Extend common courtesies: Don't be late for, cancel, or change meetings at the last minute or ignore deadlines for material requested.

Don't dismiss them or ignore them until you need them. They have a very long memory.

Don't count on them to pull you up from above or push you up from below. Theirs is a different role.

> *I never wanted to make money just for money, I needed to learn. I was a project manager for the space flight program at LTV. It was a powerful and great job. There were project engineers at my level, but*

I had the bulk of the work. I found out I was the lowest paid. That did not endear me to management. I told my boss if we looked at the situation on the basis of accomplishment, I deserved more. He agreed and encouraged me to talk to human resources. I met with a really nice man who explained I was already paid disproportionately against the curve for my age and experience. They couldn't justify paying me more. It was their rules. He told me to hang in there, "You'll get older, and we'll be able to pay you more." I started looking for a new job the next day.... I thought it was a bad idea until I had my own company and had to make similar rules. I've learned there are lots of good bonus plans, but none include a way not to pay money.

Inside your company, you're evaluated based on formal and informal assessments. The same is true when going outside. But as the informal frequently supersedes the formal internally, when you are going outside, the formal is much more prevalent.

I am my own impediment; I'm my own glass ceiling.

So an honest back-of-the-napkin review of yourself needs to be done. "Do I fear rejection/failure? Do I fail to seek help? Am I too good at what I do? Do people only see me in this niche? Am I not sure what I want? Have I aggressively pursued opportunities? Have I marketed my abilities? Have I failed to sufficiently promote myself? Are my family obligations under control? Has shyness or being too direct hurt me? Have I kept up with the right training/schooling? Do I delegate effectively? Do I lack confidence? Have I done a poor job at developing contacts? Do I have political awareness? Have I gotten exposure to other parts of the business? Do I have weak presentation skills? Am I well known enough?" These are all questions you need to ask yourself.

Sometimes the stars are not aligned in your favor.

Sometimes you're just not the "flavor of the month."

Sometimes your job is easy and you're bad at it.

I'm not promoting job hopping just for the sake of change but with the intent to grow and develop. Frequently, people get moved into a new role for two years and end up still there 13 or 23 years later—unless they manage their career.

Company policies and labor and salary grades can be strict and allow for fewer move opportunities going forward. Rigid guidelines, particularly in large companies, have a required minimum number of years in certain jobs, mandatory courses, and essential training and development—in other words, certain boxes have to be checked.

For example, if you want to end up the general manager of a GE division, you probably have to "start out as field engineer, get green belt in Six Sigma, move to master black belt, have an overseas assignment for several years, and by age 35 be a small-division general manager."

If you want to be a leader, you cannot sit at your desk doing your job, waiting until someone taps you on the shoulder and says, "Do you want to go up a level?"

I want to die on a sword of my own choosing. I'm okay with that.

I had a guy in my group who was given a huge opportunity to get out to California and make a multimillion dollar project pitch in front of a great group, and he said, "Can't do it; I've got pets." If you want to be a leader, you've got to do what it takes. You can't turn down opportunities.

Be the Boss of Your Career

Every 2.5 years, make sure that you have more complex work and added responsibility. When possible, pick good bosses. Be smart, and use human resources and executive recruiters to the degree that you can, but always remember the axiom, "Anything they can do for you, you can do for yourself even better."

What to Do If You Get Fired

Instead of fired, let's use the word one large computer firm did in its press release about 1,000 people being laid off—it was called a *skill-rebalance*.

Regardless of the euphemism, being fired or laid off is often the best possible thing that can happen to you. Many very successful CEOs have been fired at one time (Donald Trump, Michael Bloomberg, and Lee Iacocca, to name just a few well-known ones). In fact, the earlier in your career that you experience it, the better; you'll learn that it's something not to be afraid of—and your bosses can no longer hold that power over you.

There are reasons people get justifiably fired; for example, the person commits fraud, breaks agreements, is dishonest, or intentionally damages company property. Most terminations center around work duties and the economic condition of the organization. Never assume that your job is totally secure. It isn't. Your job is only as secure as the emotions of your immediate supervisor.

December is the biggest month for job terminations; January is the second. The managers who didn't want to do it before the holidays will do it in the beginning of the new year.

When the boss calls you in and delivers the news, listen carefully to exactly what is being said. Don't interrupt. Listen. If possible, write down what is being said.

Don't engage in debate. Trying to change his or her mind is usually wasted effort. If you sincerely believe that the boss is making a mistake, tell him or her. Occasionally, good bosses have been known to recognize the mistake if someone has the self-confidence to point it out.

Women—and men—should refrain from crying. Tears won't change anything. They will only embarrass everyone. Refrain from giving a detailed explanation of what you think about the boss and the boss's mother.

After the boss is finished, sit there, breath deeply, look out the window for a moment, if necessary, and get composed. Ask for specific clarification of the financial separation package.

State you'll need time to think about the offer, and talk to the boss again in a day or two. You have the option to ask for more money. The boss can only say yes or no. He or she can't fire you for asking!

When you've settled on the package, ask for the settlement offer in writing.

Go home. Don't go to a bar. Gather the family and explain the situation. Give yourself the night to feel the pain. You'll lie awake and find it hard to believe that the company has let you go. Take solace in the fact that there is nothing worse for your career than a bad fit. Now you are free to go find a good fit.

Rise early the next morning and start your job hunt.

Thoughts from a CEO friend who's been there:

> *The day you are terminated [canned, let go, fired, freed to pursue other opportunities, canceled, downsized, or dismissed], you will discover that the commuter trains still run, that the traffic doesn't care, that none of the network (or local) nightly news shows will mention your situation, that your car will still need gas, that your child (who you haven't told yet and won't think any differently toward you when you do) still needs 60 cupcakes for school tomorrow, that the dry cleaning still needs to be picked up (where you catch yourself looking at the total bill and conclude that's a luxury you'll have to cut out and you wonder about those products where you can dry clean at home and you vow to clip a coupon when you find the advertisement for it), and that the sun still goes down and the moon comes up. Unfortunately, it's a half moon, which makes you think, "Just like me—jobless—half a person."*
>
> *You might discover that your spouse has a larger profanity vocabulary than you thought, which she [or he] now chooses to spew toward your now ex-boss. You won't feel much like eating. You question your self-worth, swinging between feeling dumb and stupid. Dumb for having trusted your now ex-boss—the person whom you drank a celebratory glass of champagne with just last week on the Klondix deal; the person whose two children you bought graduation presents for, spending more than you wanted, but you felt that you needed to because you did not want to look cheap; the person you confided in about that one-time college experience; and the person for whom you worked four weekends in a row this spring instead of going to your son's soccer tournament. Stupid for finally being found out as to what a fraud you are, what a crock you provide, what worthless piece of bolshovick you are in pretending to have added any value to the organization.*

You are the director managing your career. You are in charge. You are responsible for your own career campaign. Never give away responsibility. Don't expect or ask others to do for you what you should be doing for yourself.

16

You Have Your Personal Life in Check

- Know what is important to you, and then give it at least a small amount of time every day.
- Set your ground rules.
- Get your family on board.

FREQUENTLY I HEAR SOME VERSION OF "I don't want to be the top guy because *I want to have a life—I want balance.*" People who say this will have the same discontent in their work/life balance whether they choose farming, pharmacology, or CEOdom. It's not a condition of the position; it's a condition of the decisions you make. You can have a sense of balance in your life and your home life in check regardless of your job title *if* you want it. It's your own personal adjustment.

You can be a terrific leader without sacrificing your life. You are not the first or only person who has struggled with balance. Winston Churchill referred to it as keeping one's life in "proportion." Your parents deal with it, and your children will.

In one study, 9 out of 10 people surveyed (e.g., nurses, social workers, police officers, sales people, road workers, and prison guards) say that they have stress on the job, and 70 percent of those said that it comes from juggling work and home demands.

It's true that some CEOs sleep only 4 hours a night and work most of the other 20 hours, but I know some realtors, garbage collectors, writers, oil and gas land men, and single mothers who do the same.

People choose to work to the level they want. One CEO was known for such a relentless work schedule that when it was a holiday in the U.S., he'd fly somewhere else in the world where it wasn't a holiday so that he could keep working. A different CEO, though, made it his goal to work "24-7"—that being 24 hours a week, 7 months a year.

The bulk of our imbalance or lack of proportion is due to our own choosing. People do what they want to do. One CEO friend told me, "People say, 'I'm sorry' for being late. They weren't sorry, or they wouldn't have been late. They chose to sleep later, talk on the phone longer, or whatever. They say, 'I'm sorry,' to be polite, but they don't mean it."

Being "too busy" is an excuse for not choosing.

If you've ever been on a sailboat, you may know the expression, "Keep one hand for the boat and one hand for yourself," meaning do your job on the moving craft, but take responsibility for yourself and your safety too. Having your personal life in check keeps you at the helm in your career.

I have balance because I plan it and do it. If you don't, you'll never get it. The world is so interconnected, I can have an epiphany at the top of the hill in Aspen and e-mail on the ski lift. The CEO job isn't to sit at a desk 24 hours and make sure people are doing the right thing. I have my rules, though, every day I get to zero messages and every week I'm home Friday, Saturday, and Sunday night, but even then, my mind is never actually off duty.

I sacrificed nothing I wanted or missed. If it was important to me, I would have tried to find a way to have it be part of my life.

The art of business is in some ways balancing so that everyone wins, so that everybody flourishes: customers flourish, team members flourish, shareholders flourish, the community flourishes, government flourishes. But understand that those balances are always temporary because it's human nature not to be satisfied for long. People want to know, "What have you done for me lately?" You have to continue to rebalance as the business grows.

Balance is overrated. Nothing wrong with being a one-trick pony as long as it's a good trick.

You won't impress me by working longer hours than I do.

At work, get lots done, and then leave.

What Does Having Your Home Life in Order Mean? What Does It Look Like?

If you choose to do this (because it *is* your choice), you

- Make harmonious tradeoffs with work, family, and your own time.
- Get your family on board.
- Have social and home life skills that you use in business and business skills that you use in your home life.
- Make the decision and difficult choices to ensure enjoyment, peace and contentment in your personal and professional life.
- You set a good example with your family and your colleagues.
- Listen to your mate and children when they aren't setting enough.

Know What Is Important to You and Then Give It at Least a Small Amount of Time Every Day

List what's important: work, family, children, church, charity, exercise, the arts, community, parents, continuing education, friends, fighting for justice, defending the planet, etc. Then starting as early in the day as possible (as opposed to waiting to the end), spend four minutes on every area you listed. That's right, just four minutes. Why? Four minutes is not too burdensome to find in your schedule; it's only 240 seconds. (It's sort of an umbrella that protects you from the downpour of other demands and disruptions you'll have.) It's enough time, with no interruptions, to get *something* productive completed—like one ministep toward your goal.

I am trying to get you to think about your interests in life and allocating a small chunk of time (at least) to all.

Think about it: If you spend four focused minutes with each member of your immediate family before you head to work, that's 14 minutes (figuring a spouse and, on average, 2.2 children). In each person's four minutes, you could have learned about, discussed, or decided on an activity or a schedule, shared a laughed, or solved a problem.

Do the same when you return home from work. Don't immediately look through the mail, go to change your clothes, answer the phone, get on the computer, or even pet the dog. Give another concentrated four minutes to each family member. Now, you don't want a buzzer on your wrist watch to go off so that you can head to the next person like you're speed dating.

> *I've learned that balance is much like the airlines tell us in the safety check to put on our own oxygen mask first before helping others. It only makes sense.*

> *You get a maximum of one hobby as a CEO.*

> *One of my partners loved to ride. He named his horse "Business" so that when you called his secretary, she could honestly say, "He's out on Business." I've thought of naming a boat that!*

Do not let another day go by where you missed putting time to areas of interest to you because of work tugs and priorities. Or all of a sudden, a week, months, or years go by, and you wake up one day in a fit because you've lost what and who are important to you. Everyone can find four minutes. And sometimes it turns into 14, but if not, you still have your four.

The same four-minute rule applies to people and issues at the office. "If I spent four minutes on networking [for example], that would be more action toward it than what I do now," admitted one CEO wannabee. That's typical for most of us.

Then periodically check to make sure that you're on track with interests—at this point in time. Things change. Ask yourself: "Is this the way I should be spending my precious time?" As you juggle your way through, it's okay to drop some balls as long as you chose the ones to drop.

One problem is that you can feel what you're doing at work is so important: People tell you you're doing a great job (something you don't get a lot of at home), so your priority or importance can get skewed. All the more important to consistently use the four-minute rule.

Set Your Ground Rules

When you know what's important to you, set your own personal policy. I've heard:

- "I will not be away from my wife overnight. If I can't fly in and out for a meeting in the same day, my wife goes along."
- "I'm home with my family every Friday, Saturday, and Sunday."
- "Every Sunday morning I reverse the role with my spouse, get the kids up and dressed, and make breakfast and lunch, no exceptions."
- "I won't take on a foreign assignment that keeps me and the family apart for more than two weeks."
- "I won't accept a job requiring more than a two-hour commute."
- "It's a nonnegotiable point in my contract that my wife or one family member can travel with me at any time."

These dictates from CEOs can seem a little out of reach for most of us, but as the old country and western song says, "If you don't stand for something, you'll fall for anything." At least ponder what ground rules will enable you, at this point in time, to keep your home life in check, and negotiate ways to make them happen.

A leader makes choices, and to stay a leader, you have to make the right choices.

The reality is that if you limit what you'll do for your job, management likely will limit your progression. Still, within reason, set some rules that are acceptable to you with agreement as to the times they can be broken.

Use technology. Although there are more pressured demands than ever, there is also more technology to enable you to click, drop, and drag a day's, a week's, or even a month's worth of work. This is *not* a recommendation: taking your BlackBerry to bed, which, according to a recent survey, 63 percent do.

Use services that help you save time: organizers, delivery people, pet care, lawn care, car driving services, fumigators, investigators, and massage therapy.

Stay healthy, because that's the only way you'll be able to sustain the schedule.

You don't get many sick days as the CEO.

Get Your Family on Board

Make sure that the people close to you are in sync with your dreams and goals. Tell them what's going on, and give them a defined period of time before it will be "over." You can set a broad schedule (e.g., weeks, months, or a year out), but it will be difficult to hold to, and that perturbs families.

> *My family went to the company picnic. We walked in, and a thousand eyes were on us. My teenage son about yelped, "I got to get out of here." So I had to remind him of some of the benefits he gets because he's the boss's son, and he sort of sighed and joined in.... Unfortunately, he knows that the school nurse, who's husband works for me, will write him a waiver anytime he asks.*

A small number of CEOs I interviewed were not only a part of two-career families but also two-CEO families. Others had a working spouse, and others had a nonworking spouse. One woman who resigned her vice president position to be a stay-at-home mom said, "Oh how I'd love to sit in meetings all day in an air-conditioned office with smartly dressed people instead of running around with the kids taking them to cheering practice, T-ball, dances, the dentist, the doctor, birthday parties, guitar lessons, the Spanish tutor, and the mall for shoes."

You are not the CEO of the family; we are partners [spoken by a CEO spouse].

The respect I get at the office is in the same proportion to the disrespect I get at home.

Get simpatico with your life partner, your boss, your culture, and your subordinates.

I met my wife in a bar on 25-cent draft night—but a nice college bar. Together, we've balanced career and family by making her the CEO of the house with, depending on the day of the week, me as either the nonexecutive chair or a consultant. It's a first marriage; I started off with a "trophy" wife.

My wife is a great wife. She has been a passionate supporter of my career. If you attack me, she becomes a banshee. She is very protective. We have a division of labor in the family. I make small decisions like my career. She makes big decisions like the names of our children, the schools they attend, and the church we go to.

We are very committed to a great relationship and to our young kids. We're at a time in our life when we're stretched, but we just support each other.

The biggest derailer to having your home life in check is that you have a set of personal needs that inhibit you from functioning at a high level; you have a self-discipline issue. You lack self-control with the opposite sex, booze, food, golf, steroids, gambling, pets, money, ego, debt, or drug abuse. (The United States, with less than 5 percent of the world's population, consumes more than half its drugs.)

You will be derailed if you pursue a path that gives you no personal happiness. If you're not happy in your work, you'll bring that dissatisfaction into your home time, as well as your work time.

Like confidence, integrity, the work you do, the risks you take, and the ambition you have—it's your choice. Sadly, many divorces have occurred with CEOs, C-level executives, sales people, secretaries, and janitors because all parties weren't on the same page. The sooner you get on and stay on the same page, the more work/life satisfaction you'll enjoy, the better example you'll set, and the healthier you'll be to continue to pursue your passions. It's one vicious cycle—that you control.

Conclusion: The Leadership Foursome—Confidence, Craftsmanship, Constant Communication, and Coworker Collaboration

As a leader—as a CEO—you have the keys to the car; you're the designated driver—of your team, your company, your career, and your life. Remember the feeling of getting the keys for the first time to the family car as a teen? Well, you get that same feeling every day.

When I go to work, it's like I'm going to play my favorite game every day. . . . Business travel to me is like the field trips we used to go on when we were kids.

As your parents emphasized then—and the boss today—you are responsible. You make the decisions on what to do, when, by whom, and how. Your fingerprints are all over everything—and that's exciting.

You get to identify the hill, get the troops fired up to get up the hill, and declare victory at the top of the hill. The only problem is making sure it's the right hill.

True, there are some sleepless nights. It can feel like you "have hand grenades in each hand" when you get responsibility for people's lives and investments and whether your employees' kids get braces on their teeth or not.

Few of your days are alike; you won't get bored. The diversity of challenge is significant, with you constantly experiencing things you've never had come your way before.

One day you're working "26 hours standing on your head"; the next day you have a ribbon cutting with the Queen of England as you open a new location; you attend the company picnic where you have to "kiss babies"; you have to tour Prince Andrew around your plant or golf with Supreme Court judges on one of the greatest private golf courses in the world; you take an invitation for the U.S. presidential inauguration; you stand on the track at the Indy 500; you play tennis with Monica Seles, and so on.

Yes, there will be days when you ask yourself, "What have I gotten myself into?" because you also have to deal with worker disputes or structuring or restructuring of the company, choose who to hire and who to fire, develop new products, decide which countries to distribute in, determine whether to invest in upgrading your offices or bringing information technology (IT) into your stores, and set prices, as just a sample day at the office.

There is no slam dunk. You won't get to do all that you want. You have to recognize and accept that you will never get it all done and get comfortable with that.

Chiefs are A Cross Section of Society

Some you admire; some you abhor.

> *There are few idiots who are CEOs. It's hard to be a dummy and be in that position.*

> *Some are so dumb that I wouldn't hire them for a job at minimum wage.*

Still CEOs and C-level executives are the mainstay of our country. Without them, we'd be in trouble.

It's hard to group them, but CEOs generally are overstretched, overwhelmed, overworked, and incredibly challenged because of the speed at which business takes place. (Sounds like your job today, doesn't it.)

Generally, CEOs are good, honorable, and decent. To be successful over a long time, they have to have a servant-leader mentality.

You may aspire to be chief accountant, marketing officer, finance officer, operations officer, or executive officer. Whatever it is, aim higher. You just might get it or at least more than you aimed for. If you get too much of the "good thing," you can always turn it down and walk away (usually with more money, by the way).

At the end of a long career, you'll "get" the significance of everything said in this book by the CEOs I interviewed. But why wait? Get it now at 22, 32, 42, or 52 years of age.

The takeaway to work with every day is consistency in your

- **Craftsmanship**
  - Having a good track record
  - Taking on a generalist not just a specialist mentality
  - Constantly seeking information
  - Having a fire in your belly
- **Confidence**
  - Feeling broadly adequate
  - Being decisive
  - Seeking honest feedback and improving from it
  - Being unafraid to take risks, even make mistakes
  - Managing your own career
  - Getting your family on board
- **Constant communication**
  - Being willing to stand out
  - Yet fitting in
  - Listening more than you talk
- **Coworker collaboration**
  - Being someone to trust
  - Developing others to take your job
  - Causing people to follow you even though they don't have to

All of this must be done up and down the ladder, inside and outside of the organization, with people you like and those you don't. Consistency is the key to making this happen—to get you pushed up from below and pulled up from above.

If you're competent, your future potential has never been brighter than at this time.

In 365 days, you will be a year older, or in 365 days, you will be a year older *and have* heightened confidence, improved leadership expertise, and real opportunities for promotion and advancement; you will show accelerated learning in leadership, confidence development, effective communications, and trust building as a leader. Daily practical, workable, doable action is required on a consistent basis, action that will be noticed and that supersedes formal assessment and promotion processes. Here is a years' worth of to-do-list items for you to start with today and continue every day:

- Rebuild a burnt bridge.
- Write a complimentary note to your boss, subordinate, or someone else.
- Clear up a misunderstanding that you've let remain unclear.
- Stand up for someone being belittled or attacked.
- Complete a task you've been procrastinating.
- Request a 360-degree performance evaluation.
- Go home early and spend time with your family.
- Take a job interview (for practice, confidence, etc.) outside the company.
- Take a thorny point from your 360-feedback and tackle correcting it.
- Go back to someone who told you "No" and reapproach them.
- Listen more than you talk today (watch your clock and time yourself).
- Ask questions all day as your only communication.
- Refrain from a droopy face all day.
- Physically pat your boss on the back.
- Repeat mantra such as, "I'm adequate."

- Write a complimentary note to a business reporter on an article.
- Ask a favor from someone you normally wouldn't.
- Show your humanness to someone intimidated by you.
- Write a note to someone written up in the *Wall Street Journal*.
- Volunteer to give a speech.
- Develop your accomplishment stories—24 of them.
- Create your career history book.
- Phone an old mentor and update each other.
- Start a collection of business-appropriate anecdotes, jokes, and stories.
- Inject levity into a serious business conversation.
- Recall a mistake, and write down what you learned from it.
- Recall a mistake, and check with people involved to make sure that you've rectified it.
- Look at a current problem situation from the perspective of all people involved to come up with a solution.
- Look at a current problem situation as if it were already solved to come up with a solution.
- Talk to your barber about a business problem (or someone else unrelated to the situation).
- Start work one hour earlier today.
- Before you take some action, consider the Golden Rule.
- Fix a problem.
- Take your calendar, and schedule-in personal days and activities for the rest of the year.
- Add to your financial self-worth today.
- Give acceptance to a "jerk."
- Act more confident than you feel.
- Stand ramrod straight.
- Slow down walking, moving, etc.
- Give a two-handed handshake.
- Sit asymmetrically in meetings.
- Speak up at a meeting three times more than you usually do.
- Learn some Spanish—or Scandinavian.
- Get another mentor.
- Take on a good trait that the opposite sex has.

- Ready a replacement for yourself.
- Help your boss get promoted.
- Help a subordinate get promoted.
- Accept the unacceptable for now.
- Ask for a critique.
- Read the *Economist* for a global perspective.
- Read *USA Today*, as most CEOs do.
- Say "No" when you'd typically say "Okay."
- Do some grunt work others avoid.
- Have a backwards day—do everything the opposite.
- See where your work aids in profit and loss.
- Persuade, sell.
- Speak in headlines.
- Improve your writing skills.
- Network outside your circle of acquaintances.
- Get your team to wrap up something they've been working on.
- Make someone else a star.
- Exceed expectations and requirements for a task/job.
- Repair your damaged reputation.
- Find out the boss's favorite project or the biggest thorn in his or her side, and take it on.
- Initiate cost reductions before being told.
- Make a tough decision.
- Teach a class.
- Represent the company at a community event.
- Send a note and flowers (or game tickets) to the spouse of a hardworking colleague.
- Write your life story.
- Write a list of 100 things you want to do in life before you die.
- Do one of the things on your list of 100.
- Pick a fight with your boss.
- Take a class or read a book outside your area of technical expertise.
- Write down your personal code of conduct in business.
- Self-promote with self-respect.
- Ask for a raise or promotion.

- Do something you thought impossible.
- Experiment with some new time-management technique.
- Check up on your own health.
- Remove a chip from your shoulder.
- Correct someone's performance.
- Disprove some stereotype about your race, creed, color, class, state, or church.
- Eliminate a self-defeating behavior.
- Choose a perspective that is positive and constructive versus destructive.
- Think before you talk.
- Be flexible, accommodate, but don't compromise.
- Be gutsy and take a risk.
- Fight for your people.
- Have a silent day (weekend task).
- Manage your attitude.
- Try something you've already tried, again.
- Give credit elsewhere for some good work you've done.
- Be theatrical.
- Enhance some aspect of your technical expertise.
- Give no B.S. today.
- Sit and stand up correctly.
- Pause at every entrance and exit.
- Change part of your predominate style, as tested before.
- Stand during a meeting.
- Read a historical biography (Jefferson, Lincoln, etc.).
- Read a business biography (Starbucks, etc.).
- Read a self-help book.
- Order Crane stationery cards.
- Update your résumé.
- Pay for some professional self-development out of your own pocket.
- Write a letter to the editor of your local paper.
- Write an op-ed piece.
- Go out of your way for someone who "can't help you."
- Find your "alls."
- Take your subordinate(s) to lunch.

- Take your boss to lunch.
- Take your competitor to lunch.
- Take a foe to lunch.
- Repeat your favorite 10 on this list.
- Go to the company Christmas party or picnic.
- Innovate; come up with an idea.
- Enthusiastically go with the ebb and flow of an emotional boss.
- Deliver a result.
- Be engaging.
- Give eye contact.
- Have your hearing tested.
- Butt heads without being a butthead.
- Stop whining.
- Self-start something.
- Infuse others with passion.
- Don't be flashy.
- Don't have your clothes be more interesting than you are.
- Join a professional organization.
- Step forward.
- Treat others as "adequate."
- Maintain someone's self-esteem.
- Rehearse out loud what you're going to say in a meeting before you say it.
- Role-play an exchange.
- Breathe like a yogi.
- Thank someone.
- Praise someone through a third party.
- Volunteer.
- Get your desk, files, or car organized.
- Set priorities.
- Use a "pass the salt" tone of voice.
- Use a mnemonic device to keep on track.
- Seek affinity.
- Professionally alter your clothes to fit your current weight.
- Don't read others' body language unless you ask to verify.
- Don't assume, ask.

- Practice being photographed; choose stance, clothes, etc.
- Go to a comedy club, watch the Comedy Channel, or view a comedy movie.
- Watch CNN financial news shows and watch how CEOs handle themselves on air.
- Get yourself videotaped.
- Reflect on why you're like you are (parents, schooling, socializing, etc.).
- Drive your boss to the airport.
- Fully disclose your management style.
- Fully disclose your leadership style.
- Go for a month without buying anything unnecessary.
- Seize the day or moment.
- Talk to a stranger in the elevator.
- Talk to a seatmate on a plane.
- Listen to your own outgoing voice-mail messages.
- Reread your e-mails for grammar, syntax, etc.
- Write a personal note on paper and hand deliver it.
- Wear your name tag on your right collarbone, not the left.
- Slow down speaking.
- Remember names.
- Plan spontaneity.
- Cease procrastinating firing a poor performer.
- Don't take comments personally.
- Do a salary survey for your job level.
- Do a personal public relations activity.
- Change your mind.
- Use charisma along with substance.
- Deal with an office political situation.
- Listen to a book on tape.
- Spend a day with colleagues in other job functions.
- Give 110 percent.
- Support your significant other's dream.
- Write a letter to your son or daughter about your life and what you hope for them.
- Maintain a journal.

- Give no excuses.
- Set a big goal; raise the bar.
- Give a referral to a headhunter.
- Be a mentor or coach.
- Delegate.
- Observe and write down observations.
- Plan.
- Follow your intuition.
- Discipline yourself more.
- Learn from a bad example.
- Nicely nag.
- Set a good example.
- Manage stress.
- Be yourself unless you're a "jerk."
- See around corners.
- Hire people who are smarter than you.
- Make a big play.
- Be on a board.
- Be a good social citizen.
- Vote.
- Cut through the junk in business.
- Cease regrets.
- Understand your own annual report or the report of some company in which you hold stock.
- Improve you handwriting.
- Manage a crisis.
- Check your physical appearance.
- Check in on your weight issue.
- Deal with a setback.
- Read if not a reader; talk if not a talker.
- Hang around an old person other than a family member.
- Hang around a young person other than a family member.
- Help a new hire like you wish someone would have helped you.
- Follow through on a commitment you made.
- Do something physical outside the athletic club (e.g., clean your office, clean your windows, etc.).

- Cease any negativity today.
- Talk to the janitor and the CEO on the same day in the same way.
- Stand out.
- Fit in.
- Plan and manage your first impression.
- Make some luck.
- Have a physical presence game plan when attacked.
- Don't allow distractions today.
- Follow the first four-minute rule.
- Ask three questions delving deeply with "Anything else?" or "Can you give me an example?" or "Tell me more."
- Prepare questions/comments in advance. Think them through, say them outloud. Don't let the first time you hear what you had to say come after you have already said it.
- Listen and repeat back what you heard to verify. Don't parrot back but do confirm mutual understanding.
- Play answering a question with a question exercise.
- Change any self-talk from negative to neutral or positive.
- Get away from a negative situation or person.
- Make sure there is "no bad stuff running down hill" today.
- Give a compliment to a stranger.
- Trust your gut.
- Encourage someone to be heard, even when you don't want to hear what they have to say.
- Write down all your problems.
- Make a list of people you'd like to meet.
- Put yourself in your foe's shoes.
- Think of an analogy to your stage in life.
- Keep on top of current events.
- Keep technologically current.
- Encourage all the above in others.
- Train your administrative assistant in how you want to be represented.
- Have fun; make something fun today.
- Evaluate where you are in your job, and analyze whether you should move on or stay.

- Create a financial statement for yourself.
- Go to a seminar.
- Improve your telephone technique.
- Improve your e-mail technique.
- Give this book to a friend (send it to me first; I'll autograph it).
- Switch jobs for a day with a willing colleague.
- Shadow someone doing his or her job.
- Conduct an information interview in an area of interest.
- Drive a different way to work.
- Bike, take a bus, or carpool to work.
- Use different restrooms at the office to get you in a different area.
- Read a magazine from a totally different perspective (e.g., men read *Cosmopolitan*; women read *Men's Health*).
- Count the number of smiles you see on others today versus the number of people you see.
- Give your business card to everyone today.
- Write up your dream job description so that you'll have something to aim for and compare against.
- Talk to your parents about their career successes and setbacks.
- Talk to your kids about career dreams.
- Take your parents to your work.
- Take your children to your work.
- Get an ergonomic chair.
- Write down 10 things you love about your job.
- Write down 10 things you're grateful about in life.
- Negotiate something.
- Go on a golf outing (or other sport) with a customer/colleague.
- Consult.
- Save for 6 months of personal overhead in case you lose your job.
- Travel to a foreign country.
- Get an intern.
- Recruit.
- Be on a company sports team.
- Organize a going-away party for a colleague.
- Sponsor a charity drive.

- Send a note of appreciation to the parents of a subordinate.
- Meet your CEO.
- Attend a stockholders meeting.
- Get additional power today by just taking it.
- Ask your boss what he or she wants to achieve this year.
- Ask your boss what he or she wants to maintain this year.
- Ask your boss what he or she wants to avoid this year.
- Ask questions like a reporter; use who, what, when, where, why, and how.
- Take on the task to learn the answer to the questions of what they want to achieve, maintain, avoid.
- Write down your current contact list.
- Research your competitors (companies and individuals).
- Put together a personal board of directors.
- Introduce two people who want to meet each other.
- Ask for what you want; don't hope the person will know.
- Visualize; make a movie of your future.
- Turn a goal into an action plan.
- Get a second wind.
- Facilitate getting more output from team members.
- Deliver difficult news.
- Control your temper; hold your tongue.
- Figure out what makes you tick.
- Objectively evaluate your options/opportunities with your current employer.
- Copy behaviors of others who've successfully gotten to the top.
- Market yourself through a champion who is higher up in the organization.
- Speak the language of the people who make the decisions to promote.
- Ask for help.
- Work from a 30,000-feet view; understand the whole company.
- Write a proposal for a promotion.
- Seek out victors; applaud and interview them.
- Don't wear your emotions on your sleeve.
- Develop a personal development plan.

- Create a role to fill a gap.
- Champion a company initiative with high visibility.
- Work (for now) with people you don't like.
- Prepare for a "human traffic accident."
- When you solve a problem and you make issues go away, communicate it.
- Tolerate nothing that takes you away from your goal.
- Follow-through, follow-up, don't give up.
- Have nothing be about "you" today, only others.
- Help someone do one of the "to-do" things that has helped you most.
- Send out Christmas card–type greeting in July.
- Do a random act of kindness today.
- Train your administrative assistant.
- Check customer satisfaction.
- Stuff 100 envelopes for the church social.
- Volunteer to pick up the out-of-town executive/consultant visiting the office.
- Ask a friend how you can help him or her in something he or she is doing.
- Start your spiral notebook log/journal.
- Get a personal mantra/motto.
- Meet a politician.
- Tell your kids about your day.
- Put a corporate spouse at ease in a stuffy office social gathering.
- Don't let a single buzzword slip into your conversation.
- Whistle-blow something that needs to be made known.
- Put your work into a 60-second briefing format.
- Brainstorm.
- Read; learn about China.
- Get a physical checkup.
- Remember the names today of the people you meet.
- Quantify your contributions in dollars.
- Get cross-functional experience.
- Seek out some particularly difficult people to work with.
- Tolerate fools and "stupid" people.

- Cease excessive involvement in detail.
- Motivate others.
- Take a calculated risk.
- Get out of your comfort zone.
- Be memorable.
- Be pleasantly assertive.
- Initiate cost reductions in your department.
- Compliment your CEO for the positive write-up in the *Wall Street Journal* on the company.
- Go to a social business function that you'd usually pass on.
- Outline a business article for publication.
- Write a letter to the editor of an industry trade journal.
- Ask to shadow someone for a day in a totally different field from you.
- Go to an association gathering you'd normally pass on.
- Delegate something you'd like to do yourself but know it would benefit someone else to do.
- Research competitors online, and look for a weakness your company can address.
- Take an oddball course online.
- Wear a company logo cap or shirt.
- Write a press release on your team's accomplishments.
- Represent your company at a community event.
- Read a business biography.
- Write your life story.
- Write another accomplishment story.
- Volunteer to teach a college class.
- Google yourself.
- Write a list of what you want to do in business before you die.

Literally, the day after I completed this book and it was accepted by my talented editor, Mary Glenn, I started compiling new, relevant information on the subject. To keep content alive, current, and pertinent to you, go to www.debrabenton.com for postings that will help you to continue your journey. I also welcome hearing from you. Write to debra@ debrabenton.com.

Index

About the Author

Debra Benton's focus is to "help you work differently and be different at work; to take you from promise to prominence." Her expertise has given her front-page coverage in the *Wall Street Journal* and *USA Today* (Money) and made her a welcome guest on the *Today Show, Good Morning America,* CNN, and interviewed by Diane Sawyer for CBS.

Conde Nast Portfolio magazine described Benton as one of the "top five executive coaches to have on speed dial."

Debra has written for the *Harvard Business Review,* the *Wall Street Journal,* and has been the bestselling, award-winning author of eight books.

She is a popular keynote speaker and leadership consultant. A few of her clients are: General Electric, American Express, United Airlines, Time Warner, McKinsey & Company, Verizon, Novartis Pharmaceuticals, Kraft Foods, Dell Inc., Pratt & Whitney, Lockheed Martin, and the U.S. Border Patrol, as well as individuals from Hollywood to the Washington Beltway.

Benton lives with her husband Rodney Sweeney, a retired cowboy and ranch manager, in Colorado.

Visit Debra at www.debrabenton.com.